"It is near-impossible for this book not to touch o[...]
beautiful, powerful and passionate, and tells a s[...]
giveness, love and hope. In *Dreamtalk*, Sheen[...]
and Gail Robinson provide very unique, but [...]
on traumatic brain injury. Understanding this [...]
ing personal stories into plans to ensure the [...]
represents the art of neurorehabilitation. Th[...]
clinicians and academics with an interest in [...]
anyone who wants to learn more about what [...]

     – **Dr. Rudi Coetzer, Consult**[...]
      Head of the North W[...]
     Betsi Cadwaladr University Health Board,
            NHS Wales, UK

"One fateful day in February 1999 Sheena McDonald sustained a very severe brain injury, changing the trajectory of her life. This book provides a poignant account of her recovery from this traumatic event. Combining Sheena's account with that of her partner and her neurorehabilitation specialist enables the reader to gain a holistic insight into recovery from brain injury. This book is vital reading for any professional involved in neurorehabilitation, and the individuals and families touched by brain injury. It reminds the reader that every person affected by brain injury can make a remarkable recovery. Life may not be the same as before, but there is hope."

     – **Dr. Anita Rose, Consultant Clinical Neuropsychologist,**
        The Raphael Hospital, Kent, UK

Rebuilding Life After Brain Injury

Rebuilding Life After Brain Injury: Dreamtalk tells the survival story of Sheena McDonald, who in 1999 was hit by a police van and suffered a very severe brain injury. Sheena's story is told from her own, personal standpoint and also from two further unique and invaluable perspectives. Allan Little, a BBC journalist and now Sheena's husband, describes both the physical and mental impact of the injury on himself and on Sheena. Gail Robinson, Sheena's neuropsychological rehabilitation specialist, provides professional commentaries on Sheena's condition, assessment and recovery process.

The word *Dreamtalk*, created by Allan to describe Sheena's once "hallucinogenic state", sets the tone for this book. It humanises and contextualises the impact of brain injury, providing support and encouragement for patients, professionals and families. It presents exclusive insights into each stage of recovery, spanning coma, altered consciousness, posttraumatic amnesia and rehabilitation; all showing how Sheena has defied conventional clinical expectations and made an exceptional recovery.

This book is valuable reading to those who have suffered a brain injury and also to professionals such as neurologists, neuropsychologists, physiotherapists, occupational therapists and speech therapists working in the field.

Sheena McDonald is a British radio and TV journalist.

Allan Little is a British radio and TV journalist working for the BBC, and co-author of *The Death of Yugoslavia* (1995).

Gail Robinson is a Consultant Clinical Neuropsychologist and Associate Professor at the Queensland Brain Institute & School of Psychology, the University of Queensland in Brisbane, Australia. She specialises in detailed single-case studies.

After Brain Injury: Survivor Stories

Series Editor: Barbara A. Wilson

This new series of books is aimed at those who have suffered a brain injury, and their families and carers. Each book focuses on a different condition, such as face blindness, amnesia and neglect, or diagnosis, such as encephalitis and locked-in syndrome, resulting from brain injury. Readers will learn about life before the brain injury, the early days of diagnosis, the effects of the brain injury, the process of rehabilitation and life now. Alongside this personal perspective, professional commentary is also provided by a specialist in neuropsychological rehabilitation, making the books relevant for professionals working in rehabilitation such as psychologists, speech and language therapists, occupational therapists, social workers and rehabilitation doctors. They will also appeal to clinical psychology trainees and undergraduate and graduate students in neuropsychology, rehabilitation science and related courses who value the case study approach.

With this series, we also hope to help expand awareness of brain injury and its consequences. The World Health Organization has recently acknowledged the need to raise the profile of mental health issues (with the WHO Mental Health Action Plan 2013–2020) and we believe there needs to be a similar focus on psychological, neurological and behavioural issues caused by brain disorder, and a deeper understanding of the importance of rehabilitation support. Giving a voice to these survivors of brain injury is a step in the right direction.

Published titles:

A Different Perspective of Life After Brain Injury
A Tilted Point of View
Christopher Yeoh

Locked-In Syndrome After Brain Damage
Living Within My Head
Barbara A. Wilson, Paul Allen, Anita Rose and Veronika Kubickova

For more information about this series, please visit: www.routledge.com/After-Brain-Injury-Survivor-Stories/book-series/ABI

Rebuilding Life After Brain Injury

Dreamtalk

Sheena McDonald, Allan Little and Gail Robinson

Routledge
Taylor & Francis Group

LONDON AND NEW YORK

First published 2019
by Routledge
2 Park Square, Milton Park, Abingdon, Oxon OX14 4RN

and by Routledge
711 Third Avenue, New York, NY 10017

Routledge is an imprint of the Taylor & Francis Group, an informa business

© 2019 Sheena McDonald, Allan Little & Gail Robinson

British Library Cataloguing-in-Publication Data
A catalogue record for this book is available from the British Library

Library of Congress Cataloging-in-Publication Data
Names: McDonald, Sheena, 1954- author.
Title: Rebuilding life after brain injury : dreamtalk / Sheena
    McDonald, Allan Little & Gail Robinson.
Description: Milton Park, Abingdon, Oxon ; New York, NY :
    Routledge, [2019] |
Series: After brain injury: survivor stories | Includes bibliographical
    references and index.
Identifiers: LCCN 2018056878 (print) | LCCN 2019000573 (ebook)
    | ISBN 9780429470769 (Ebook) | ISBN 9781138600720 (hbk) |
    ISBN 9781138600737 (pbk) | ISBN 9780429470769 (ebk)
Subjects: LCSH: McDonald, Sheena, 1954- | Brain—Wounds and
    injuries. | Brain damage—Patients—Great Britain—Biography.
Classification: LCC RD594 (ebook) | LCC RD594 .M33 2019 (print)
    | DDC 617.4/81044092 [B]—dc23
LC record available at https://lccn.loc.gov/2018056878

ISBN: 978-1-138-60072-0 (hbk)
ISBN: 978-1-138-60073-7 (pbk)
ISBN: 978-0-429-47076-9 (ebk)

Typeset in Times New Roman
by Swales & Willis Ltd, Exeter, Devon, UK

For all who hope to recover

For all with the courage to care

And for clinicians brave enough to navigate.

Contents

Figures

Tables

Series foreword

After Brain Injury: Survivor Stories was launched in 2014 to meet the need for a series of books aimed at those who have suffered a brain injury and their families and carers. Brain disorders can be life-changing events with far-reaching consequences. However, in the current climate of cuts to funding and service provision for neuropsychological rehabilitation, there is a risk that people whose lives have been transformed by brain injury may be left feeling isolated with little support.

So many books on brain injury are written for academics and clinicians and filled with technical jargon, and so are of little help to those directly affected. Instead, this series offers a much-needed personal insight into the experience, as each book is written by a survivor, or group of survivors, who are living with the very real consequences of brain injury. Each book focuses on a different condition, such as face blindness, amnesia and neglect, or diagnosis, such as encephalitis and locked-in syndrome, resulting from brain injury. Readers will learn about life before the brain injury, the early days of diagnosis, the effects of the brain injury, the process of rehabilitation and life now.

Alongside this personal perspective, professional commentary is also provided by a specialist in neuropsychological rehabilitation. The historical context, neurological state of the art, and data on the condition, including the treatment, outcome and follow-up, will also make these books appealing to professionals working in rehabilitation, such as psychologists, speech and language therapists, occupational therapists, social workers and rehabilitation doctors. This series will also be of interest to clinical psychology trainees and undergraduate and graduate students in neuropsychology, rehabilitation science and related courses who value the case study approach as a complement to the more academic books on brain injury.

With this series, we also hope to help expand awareness of brain injury and its consequences. The World Health Organization has recently acknowledged the need to raise the profile of mental health issues (with the WHO Mental Health Action Plan 2013–2020) and we believe there needs to be a similar focus on psychological, neurological and behavioural issues caused by brain disorder, and a deeper understanding of the importance of rehabilitation support. Giving a voice to these survivors of brain injury is a step in the right direction.

Professor Barbara A. Wilson, OBE, PhD, DSc,
CPsychol, FBPsS, FmedSC, AcSS
Clinical Neuropsychologist
January 2017

Note

This book incorporates three points of view: that of Sheena, her husband Allan, and Sheena's clinical neuropsychologist, Gail Robinson. To distinguish between the different speakers, three different styles of font have been used, as follows:

Sheena – serif; Allan – *italics*; Gail – sans-serif

Preface

Twenty years ago I suffered a very severe head-injury. The clinical shorthand for this is TBI – traumatic brain injury. Today, I am a non-conformist TBI survivor. I seem to have defied conventional clinical expectations.

I am not typical – which makes me typical. Every brain injury is unique. I was 44, a successful freelance broadcast journalist, working in radio and television in and from the United Kingdom for the BBC, Channel 4, STV, ITV and numerous non-broadcast contractors. What some viewers remember me for is reading the news on Scottish Television or Channel 4 – but my work took me far and wide, and I covered a wide range of current affairs: art, religion, education, business and war. That was my life before the injury.

I was knocked down when crossing the road in Islington in London, in February 1999, by a police van being driven on the wrong side of the road. My injury was to the head and it was very severe. So my life after that has developed variously. Formally, I am a statistic in the folder labelled RTA – road traffic accidents.

Severe and very severe head-injuries can be externally generated as mine was – in or by motor vehicles, or by falling or being violently attacked (traumatic brain injuries or TBIs); they can also be internally generated, by some form of stroke or similar neurological event. Together, these categories are designated as acquired brain injuries – ABIs. Each case is different, but many share elements which enable professional and lay carers to assist the sufferer to recover a greater or lesser degree of what they have lost: their short-term and long-term memories; their ability to lay down new memories; their ability to use language – and much more.

Two voices that help to tell my story are such people – one professional and one lay. Gail Robinson is Associate Professor of Clinical

Neuropsychology at the University of Queensland in Brisbane. In 1999, she worked at the National Hospital for Neurology and Neurosurgery in London. The second voice is that of Allan Little. He had been my partner for some five years, and was working as a television and radio foreign correspondent for the BBC. In 1999, he was based in Moscow.

Over the five years following the injury, he and I met regularly with Gail Robinson, whose professional guidance and support was vital to my long and slow recovery. Gail now lives and works in Australia, while Allan and I are based in the UK.

However any form of brain injury is acquired, the immediate sufferer is usually the last person to become aware of the event, the subsequent condition and its long-term implications. It is the family and friends who agonize over their loved one's comatose body and addled mind. And brain-injury is still viewed with fear.

Surely anyone who survives such colossal damage can never be the same person, far less be able to learn and earn, live and love, contribute and participate, initiate and develop.

I suffered a very severe brain-injury at a time when I was sufficiently in the public eye for it to make headlines. The fact that I am writing this (without the help of a ghost-writer) may, of course, suggest that the injury cannot have been so severe.

I do not seek to offer false hope to the relatives of other sufferers – simply to suggest that conventional professional wisdom does not always construe situations correctly. It is impossible to generalise about brain-injury. Every single case is different. There are a few common themes:

- Any and every recovery takes time – far longer than any broken bone; longer, too, than many heart conditions or forms of cancer.
- Relatives and carers must brace themselves: they are in it for the long haul.
- The eventual results may or may not be fulfilling and satisfactory.

Recovering from TBI or ABI: there is a cadre of neurologists that believes that "recovery" is an unachievable outcome for the severely brain-injured.

This is my story.

Chapter 1

What happened?

The twenty-sixth of February 1999 was an important day for me, but I remember very little about it. My life changed significantly – not through graduation, or marriage, or bereavement, but by being hit by a police van driving down the wrong side of the road.

It happened at the end of what had been a busy day. I woke in my house in London, and set off to catch an early flight to Glasgow, where I was to chair a one-day political conference about how the coming Scottish Parliament would improve opportunities and life for women in Scotland.

On the way out to the airport, the taxi broke down. Unusual, and infuriating. I could not miss this flight. I am told I hitched a lift – I have no memory of this – and did catch the plane. I told the assembled women at the conference about the trip to the airport, and finished the story – ". . . and I thought this was going to be the worst day of my life!"

At the end of the day, I travelled back to London, where I had a meeting with the editor of a BBC political programme which I was due to present in two weeks' time – something I had done regularly. I also had a meeting with Channel 4 News – a regular source of work as a presenter and reporter. My main activity that evening was to attend a lecture at BAFTA, the British Academy of Film and Television Arts, to be given by the retiring head of the British Board for Film Censorship (as it was then called), James Ferman. I asked a question from the floor during the subsequent discussion. After the event, we continued the conversation in the bar. I had a glass of white wine, and we discussed the nature and purpose of censorship.

At eleven o'clock the bar closed. I turned down the offer of a lift from James Ferman and his wife, and elected to go back to Islington by taxi. I retain no memory of the next hour, so what follows is factually based conjecture.

When I reached Islington it was just before midnight. The regular Friday night tattoo of police-car sirens filled the air. As ever, in a built-up area, it was impossible to tell where the noise was coming from. Having reached the Angel crossroads, the taxi was stuck in a double lane of gridlocked traffic. I got out and paid the driver, intending to walk the remaining quarter-mile home. I had done this before: I resent paying to sit in a motionless cab. I started to cross the road between the stationary cars. Halfway across, I looked left, to where traffic going westwards would be approaching.

There was nothing coming. It was safe to cross. So I stepped into the road and straight into the path of a police vehicle – a van. It was travelling in an easterly direction – on the wrong side of the road.

BANG!

I have no recollection of being hit. I have met no eyewitnesses. I was wearing a winter coat, trousers and flat shoes. The police driver was steering two tons of metal, at a certain speed.

Aside from the driver and passenger, no-one saw exactly what happened. Plenty of folk saw the immediate aftermath, including a couple of off-duty nurses and a doctor on his way home. By complete coincidence, he was the son of someone my mother met at a party some time later. He spoke to his mother on the phone the following day: "I think she was dead, or will die."

Years later, I read the incident report by PC Bryce of Scratchwood Police who attended the scene on the night. He relied on people who were there and what they said:

> Police van on call filtering through traffic. Saw pedestrian on near side stepping out therefore moved away. Continued to walk out into middle of road, looking away from van therefore started to brake. Collided with pedestrian and carried short distance on front of van before falling beneath it. Van reversed away from pedestrian immediately. Pedestrian driven over by van itself?? Accident investigators estimate maximum speed 20–25 mph.

The immediate consequence of suffering a profound blow on the head from a potentially lethal weapon travelling at some speed is not a fast replay of one's previous life. My life did not flash before me. I experienced no glimpse of "the next life". Many weeks later, I mentioned this to Allan. He sniffed. "You didn't die," he pointed out. But I came close.

Some years later, I requested notes from the three hospitals where I was treated – and police-records, such as they were – and I questioned my family and Allan in order to try to build an understanding of what happened.

I was taken by ambulance to University College London's Accident and Emergency Unit where I lapsed into a coma. This was assessed at Level 6 on the Glasgow Coma Scale.

The hospital notes record:

> This 44-year-old lady was admitted to the Intensive Care Unit following a road traffic accident in which she was a pedestrian hit by a van travelling at approximately 30 mph. She sustained a significant head injury, a peri-orbital fracture plus multiple facial fractures and an oblique fracture of her left middle finger. She required intubation in the A&E Department and following a CT scan of her head was transferred to the Intensive Care Unit.

The "peri-orbital fracture" locates where the van hit me, just above my right eye.

Intubation, or endotracheal intubation (a procedure for taking over mechanical control of the most basic functions, using tubes), and assisted ventilation were carried out, apparently with some difficulty. First, I had to be paralysed. I am told that this can be distressing when one is fully conscious, but I was completely unconscious. Recovery begins in a very fundamental way.

Those who saw me soon after the injury told me much later that my physical injuries looked dramatic. My eyes were swollen shut (and when they were prised open, the whites were bright red, and swollen). I was bruised all over my body.

My brother, Rod, was the first blood relative to see me. Years later he shared his memories.

"It was a week after my 40th birthday. Sheena had come to Peterborough on my birthday to celebrate. I remember getting the phone-call from my dad about seven o'clock the morning after she was knocked down. My wife Diane and I got the next train to London and went straight to the hospital. Sheena was in a deep coma. She was unrecognisable. Her head was black and blue and swollen to twice the normal size and there was a large hole in the right side of her face where her eye should have been. I was in shock – I was numb. I could not see how Sheena could survive this.

"My mum and dad arrived later in the day on the train from Edinburgh. I remember my dad was in tears – I had never seen my dad cry before."

My mother's recollection is vivid:
"If the police call at 4 a.m. you can be sure than something catastrophic has happened. We caught a train early in the morning to London to be paged by the police at Kings Cross Station. They drove us to the hospital, and for several days were very attentive (admission of guilt?). "Sheena was unconscious and totally unrecognisable. Her face was so damaged and swollen that her eyes seemed to have disappeared. She had an oxygen mask on and there was a tangle of other pipes."
Mum was to spend the next four weeks at my bedside, but I remember nothing of her being there.
Twenty-four hours after the injury, Allan arrived.

I was sleeping late. Moscow is three hours ahead, which, since the main evening news was then aired at 9 p.m. in the UK, meant that it was after midnight before I'd finished work. I'd had a drink with colleagues after working late and had got back to my Moscow flat in the small hours, finally getting to bed probably not long before Sheena was crossing that fateful road.

The call woke me from a deep sleep and I answered it groggily. To my surprise I heard the voice of my oldest and closest friend, Alan. He was ringing from his home in Scotland. Like me he'd made a career in the media and was well connected at Channel 4, and he'd heard what had happened from friends there.

I greeted him as cheerfully as I could in my under-slept state, but I could tell there was something not right. He didn't waste time on pleasantries. "I've got bad news," he said, straight off. "Sheena's been in an accident. It looks quite serious."

These were the last days of the old world before instant internet communications. I didn't even have a mobile phone. Alan gave me a landline number in London which he said was a visitors' room in the hospital Sheena had been admitted to. I asked Alan to call my parents and tell them what had happened. Alan had known my parents since we were teenagers and they liked him. I knew I couldn't face breaking this news to them so asked Alan to do that for me.

I rang the number Alan had given me, and Sheena's brother Rod answered. He told me what he knew: that it had been a police van driving on the wrong side of the road. He'd seen Sheena and it looked bad.

I don't remember much more. Your mind goes into freefall and you find yourself incapable of coherent thought. I knew I had to get back to London but found myself unable even to organise the packing of a bag.

My phone rang again. It was my sister Nina. She was crying and the sound of her voice broke me too. I heard myself sobbing and saying over and over again "I don't know what to do." I asked her to reassure our parents that I was fine and that everything was going to be OK. I knew I had to get back to London that day. But there was a problem. My passport was locked in the Russian Ministry of Foreign Affairs, because my visa and work permit were due for renewal. It was a Saturday. I had no idea what to do.

I rang my friend Rob Parsons, a fellow BBC Moscow Correspondent and (unlike me) a fluent Russian speaker. I told him I had to get home to London – today. Rob contacted a duty diplomat in the British Embassy – a young Scot who I would meet much later and to whom I will always be grateful – and he arranged for my passport to be liberated from Russia's bureaucracy. I would also need an exit visa – the process normally took several days, but the young Scot arranged for one to be issued at the airport.

Rob drove me to the airport, steered me in a haze of grief and disbelief through the nightmare bureaucracy of the Russian emigration system, gave me the name of a London hotel the BBC had booked for me, and put me on the plane.

No flight I have ever taken has seemed more interminable. I wanted desperately to get to London but after three hours, as the plane began its descent and shuddered through the cloud cover, I was full of foreboding. It had been hours since I'd spoken to Rod. Sheena's condition had been very precarious. Suddenly I didn't want the flight to end at all, for fear of what I might find when I landed. I knew that I would soon learn whether Sheena was still alive. It terrified me.

This is how the journey starts for those closest to the brain injury survivor. It's a journey that changes the trajectory of your life, your priorities, your values, your hopes and ambitions, your sense of who you are in the world, and your relationship with those around you. But you don't know it yet. Other bad things might have happened in your life but there has always been a back-to-normal resolution. This, I would learn, would be different. A barrier had descended cutting Sheena and me off from our past lives. I didn't know it yet but there would be no going back to the way things had been before that day; no "normal" to go back to. You are entering a new and unknown country, with an unfamiliar language and no map.

I took a cab from Gatwick. I had no luggage with me. It was close to midnight and the streets were cold and quiet. The hospital entrance was in a dark side-street off the Tottenham Court Road. There were a couple of homeless men sprawled by the doorstep surrounded by cigarette butts

*and empty beer cans. I had to step over them to get in. A central London
Accident and Emergency Department on a Saturday night is full of sullen
or angry drunks with varying minor injuries – fat lips, broken jaws, split
heads. The reception area was desolate and soulless: bloodied clothes
discarded, puddles of muddy water on the floor. An ambulance crew
swept through and I stopped one of them. He directed me up a flight of
stairs to a little landing. There were two doors. A sign above one said
"Visitors Room". This was the room where Rod had been when I'd spoken to him earlier. I remember thinking "Was it really only today? It
already feels like an age ago".*

*The sign above the other door said "Intensive Care Unit". You
entered through double swing-doors. I went in, and, surprised that there
was no ante-room, found myself standing by the bed of a woman I didn't
know who, I learned later, had contracted malaria on holiday in Africa
and had ignored the symptoms until it was too late.*

*There were four beds in the room; not really beds at all, but gurneys,
functional platforms designed to give the greatest possible access for
the application of urgent medical intervention. Sheena was in the one
furthest from the door. She lay covered in a single white sheet. The room
was hot. There were no windows and no natural light. I would learn in
the days that lay ahead that there was no day or night in this room, just
a continual here-and-now of unchanging artificial light – and vital artificial life support.*

*It surprised me too that the night-shift nurses, when they spoke to
each other, spoke loudly, casually. Why weren't they whispering? It
seemed an offence against the time of night and I wondered why they
didn't take more care not to rouse their sleeping patients. My learning curve was steepening. None of the patients, I quickly realised, was
capable of being roused. They were all comatose. That's why they
were here.*

*At first I didn't recognise Sheena. I thought there had been a mis-
take; that it wasn't her. She was unrecognisable. Her face was enormous,
swollen and discoloured, red and blue in patches, and her eyelids were
a violent distressed crimson. Her chest rose and fell to the pace of the
ventilator that was moving air through her lungs by tubes that twisted her
mouth into a grimace. I saw that the right-hand-side of her abdomen was
also a vivid black and blue, from her head, down her torso, to her knees.
Wires were taped to her face, her arms, her hands and across her chest.
Behind her, black and green screens monitored her heartbeat, her blood
pressure, her breathing.*

Her hair was swept back from her forehead and this gave me my moment of recognition. The hairline was hers. And the feet protruding from the sheet at the bottom of the bed were also distinctively, recognisably her own. The hole above her right eye that Rod had reported earlier in the day had been hastily stitched up by a maxillofacial surgeon. He'd worked well, piecing the the torn and swollen tissue back together, reassembling the contours of her face as best he could, but he'd had to work quickly alongside trauma surgeons performing more urgent, life-saving tasks, and the scar that would be left above her eye would need attention, and more surgery, later.

"Maxillofacial": relating to the jaw and face, from the Latin maxillla, *meaning "jaw"; the first new word in an alienating and clinical new lexicon that would now enter our lives and help steer us through this bewildering terrain.*

I stayed into the small hours just staring. The nurses – there was a ratio of one nurse to one patient – were kindly but matter-of-fact. It was all in a day's work to them. I started to talk to her. I was scared by the idea that inside her head there would be some knowledge of what had happened, some flickering consciousness of the predicament and danger she was in, and that she would be feeling fear.

"There's been an accident," I said.

"You've had a bang on the head and that's why you're a bit groggy, but the medics are on it, they've had a good look and everything is going to be OK. It'll just take a bit of time. You're going to be fine."

I repeated this over and over, knowing it was a lie.

The nurses let me do this, indulging my need. They knew perfectly well – though I didn't – that it wasn't making a blind bit of difference to Sheena, who couldn't hear a thing, but I see now that they thought it was probably a good thing for me. And it was. It was my first tentative act in the role that I was now assuming – though again I didn't yet know it: the role of principal carer.

In the middle of the night the nurse assigned to Sheena's care decided, I think, that it would be better for me to get some rest. "She's heavily sedated," he said. "She's not really aware of anything. It's probably better for you to get some sleep. You'll need your energy in the coming days."

I didn't know then what I would learn later - that the part of her brain where fear and anxiety normally reside were so badly bruised and swollen, compressed against the confining cage of her skull, that they were just not functioning. Fear, anxiety, silent terror – these emotions were neurologically impossible for her.

Seeing, I think, that I was bewildered, the nurse touched my arm as though to reassure me. "I was on duty when they brought her in last night," he said. "It was really touch and go. Her throat tissue was so swollen that we had trouble 'intubating' her..." – "intubation": the second new word of my now medicalised life – "... and we were a few seconds away from doing a tracheotomy, cutting a hole in her throat so that we could get the tubes into her lungs. She was in a very bad way. Tonight, I'm amazed how stable she is. I'm not a doctor, but I've been in intensive care for a few years, and you just get a feeling sometimes. And when I came in tonight and saw her I thought – yeah, this one's going to make it."

Chapter 2

Was it that bad?

Traumatic brain injury

The acronyms that relate to head-injury – TBI (traumatic brain injury), ABI (acquired brain injury), MRI (magnetic resonance imaging), CAT- or CT-scanning (computerized axial tomography, an X-ray procedure which records soft tissue as well as bone, and detects bleeding), PTA (post-traumatic amnesia) – were unknown to me before the injury, as they are to most sufferers and carers. Later, I read that "the longer the length of coma and PTA, the poorer will be the outcome". I was deemed to have suffered a "very severe head injury", and the medical profession's expectations accorded to that.

What is a traumatic brain injury?

An external force to the head causes a traumatic brain injury (TBI). The most common type of TBI is a "closed TBI", which occurs when the external force causes the brain to move within the skull. For instance, a closed TBI occurs when someone falls or is involved in a motor vehicle accident, like in Sheena's case. By contrast, an "open TBI" occurs when an object such as a bullet penetrates the skull. The mechanics of a TBI can be understood by knowing that the brain is similar in consistency to a firm jelly, and it is enclosed in a hard bony casing, the skull, with any space left filled with cerebrospinal fluid, which cushions the brain and provides buoyancy to protect it in everyday life. A TBI is an extraordinary blow that far exceeds the force of bouncing and jolting that occurs during our typical daily movements. What does this mean? The sheer force of the blow and impact of a moving vehicle with a relatively stationary person is a "David and Goliath" battle. It would be remarkable if there were to be no consequences from the impact of a TBI.

TBI defined: primary and secondary damage

How exactly does a TBI affect the brain? A TBI can result in *primary damage* to a very specific (or *focal*) part of the brain, with the frontal and temporal areas most vulnerable to trauma (Walsh, 1991). *Primary focal injuries* can include skull fractures (linear – skull is "split"; depressed – skull is "dented"), contusions or "bruising" at the impact *coup* site or on the opposite *contrecoup* side of the brain and haemorrhages (bleeds within the brain – intracranial – or above/below the coverings of the brain – epidural, subdural or subarachnoid bleeds) (see Figure 2.1).

A TBI can also result in *widespread damage*, which affects a greater number of areas and is also known as *diffuse axonal injury*. Diffuse axonal injury

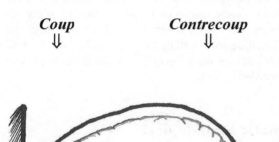

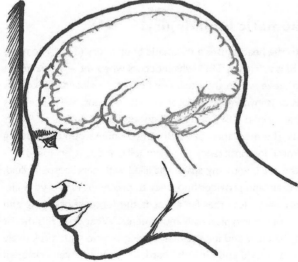

Figure 2.1 Mechanisms of a TBI

Table 2.1 The Glasgow Coma Scale (GCS: www.glasgowcomascale.org);
Sheena's GCS in February and March 1999

			Date GCS assessed 27/2	3/3	6/3
EYE OPENING	Spontaneous	4			*
(4 points)	Responds to speech	3			
	Responds to pain	2		*	
	None	1	*		
VERBAL RESPONSE	Oriented to time, place and person	5			
(5 points)	Confused and some disorientation	4			*
	Produces words (inappropriate to context)	3			
	Produces sound (incomprehensible)	2		*	
	None	1	*		
MOTOR RESPONSE	Responds and obeys commands	6			*
(6 points)	Moves to localized pain	5			
	Flexion withdrawal from pain	4	*		
	Abnormal flexion	3			
	Abnormal extension	2		*	
	None	1			
Total = 15	**Sheena's GCS in A&E = 6/15**		**6/15**	**6/15**	**14/15**

occurs when the white matter of the brain, or axons of the nerve cells, are disturbed and the electrical signal between neurons is disrupted. Clinicians often use the analogy of "stretching" a wire so it shears or is torn; this results in electrical signals not being efficiently transferred. Implicated in diffuse axonal injury is *secondary damage* due to the release of other chemicals into the brain. At this point, I will mention several specific terms that are common in TBIs. *Secondary injuries* may include hypoxia (lack of oxygen to the brain), multi-focal microvascular injuries (ischaemia), cerebral swelling (oedema), post-traumatic hydrocephalus (accumulation of cerebrospinal fluid in the brain) and post-traumatic seizures (caused by disruption to brain electrical activity) (for overview see Barker, Gibson and Robinson, 2018).

Neuroimaging of TBI can be nonspecific or give generalised indicators. As for Sheena, on admission to A&E computerized tomography (CT) is typically the first technique used to ascertain primary damage, including contusions, haemorrhages and skull fractures. This is how Sheena's right maxillofacial fracture was confirmed, as well as an intracranial haemorrhage in the left occipital lobe. At later stages, magnetic resonance imaging (MRI) can reveal subtler or finer-grained damage, including white matter changes and diffuse axonal injury. For a detailed scientific investigation of neuroimaging the extent of diffuse axonal injury following TBI, and the relationship of this with memory and other aspects of cognition, see the study led by Dr. David Sharp and Sheena's Consultant Neurologist, Dr. Richard Greenwood (Kinnunen *et al.*, 2010).

TBI signs and severity

An altered state of consciousness is the most consistent clinical characteristic following TBI. This can include a loss of consciousness, memory disturbance or changes in the functions of the brain. Loss of consciousness means that a person lacks awareness of themselves or the environment, which can range from a partial loss (or disorientation) to a complete loss, in which case an individual may appear to be asleep. Memory disturbance can be for events prior to the TBI (retrograde amnesia) or for events after the TBI (anterograde amnesia; see Figure 2.2). In broad terms these changes can disturb physical functions such as muscle tone, balance or mental functions, the latter impacting cognition (or thinking skills), behaviour and emotions.

Measuring the level of consciousness is currently the best indicator of injury severity and outcome. The two clinical measures that are most frequently used are (1) the depth and duration of coma and (2) the duration of post-traumatic amnesia (PTA). These two measures correlate with the severity of the diffuse brain injury sustained and subsequent functional outcome (see Ponsford, Sloan and Snow, 1995).

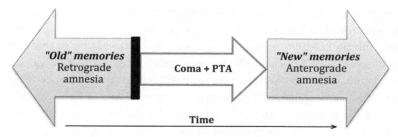

Figure 2.2 Memory disturbance and TBI (indicated by solid black vertical line)

Table 2.2 Clinical indicators of severity in traumatic brain injury (Sheena in **bold**)

Measure	Severity classification				
	Mild	Moderate	Severe	Very severe	Extremely severe
Glasgow Coma Scale	13–15	9–12	**3–8**	–	–
Loss of consciousness	<30min	30min–24hrs	**>24hrs**	–	–
Post-traumatic amnesia	<24hrs	1–7 days	>7 days	1–4 weeks	**>4 weeks**

Note: Table adapted from McCrea, *et al.* (2014) with added information from Jennett and Teasdale (1981).

Clinical measures of severity: coma

The Glasgow Coma Scale (GCS; Teasdale and Jennett, 1974) assesses neurological status after TBI. According to the GCS, coma is defined as an absence of eye opening, failure to obey commands and failure to give any comprehensible verbal response (GCS <9; see Table 2.1). When Sheena was admitted to A&E at the University College London Hospital (UCLH) early in the hours of 27 February 1999, her GCS was 6/15. A complication of measuring consciousness with the GCS is that pain medication (sedation) and inserting a tube to aid breathing (intubation) can make it difficult to obtain accurate responses from a patient. Sheena was both sedated and intubated upon admission, which was crucial for survival but likely confounded the measurement of consciousness. Regardless, several days later, on 3 March, Sheena remained in a coma with a GCS of 6/15. However, by 6 March her GCS had dramatically improved to 14/15, her only poor response given to the orientation questions. This means that Sheena could open her eyes spontaneously, move her body when asked and could talk, but she did not know exactly who she was, where she was or what time it was (see Table 2.1). From this point, Sheena remained at a GCS score of 14/15 for several weeks, consistently losing one point because she was disoriented.

Clinical measures of severity: post-traumatic amnesia (PTA)

A second widely used clinical indicator of TBI severity is PTA duration. In 1943, Symonds and Russell described PTA as the disturbance to memory function after TBI. The duration of PTA includes the period of coma and the state of clouded consciousness in which there is an inability to remember ongoing events. It is the time from injury to the start of continuous memory for ongoing events although individuals often experience "islands of memory" rather than continuous memory (Roberts, 1994). The length of the PTA period can be minutes, hours, days, weeks or months (Iverson and Lange, 2011). Duration of PTA predicts performance on a range of cognitive tests (Shores, 1989), and is related to functional outcome and post-injury vocational status (Stambrook et al., 1990). There is no agreement about which indicator (GCS or PTA) is better, but many clinicians are pragmatic and reflect the view of Wilson and colleagues (1993); that is, the GCS score and PTA duration are both related to injury severity but reflect different patterns of damage and hence are complementary measures. For injury severity classification, as indicated by coma depth and duration, and PTA duration, see Table 2.2.

In Sheena's case, both the depth and duration of coma and the duration of PTA were helpful. As a clinician, I search for injury details and the GCS score before I meet a patient. This guides my planning for neuropsychological assessment and then I assess and note, or I continue to measure, PTA. It is duration of PTA that I consider with greater weight when I think about injury severity and long-term prognosis. All clinicians "know" that a patient in the Moderate, Severe or Very/Extremely severe categories is unlikely to fully recover or return to previous life roles. Before I met Sheena, I saw the GCS score of 6 and my first thought was "Oh boy, we are in for a long and rocky road to recovery."

My mother insists that she knew from the start I would get better. She told me that she sat with me in the early weeks for whole days: "The coma lasted for several days, and then the chief nurse told me to speak loudly – 'She might respond to your voice.' I was told that I said, 'Get a grip, Sheena.' Then I felt guilty. But maybe you did respond."

References

Barker, M.S., Gibson, E.C. and Robinson, G.A. (2018). *Acquired Brain Injury (Stroke and TBI) in Later Life*. Oxford: Oxford Research Encyclopedia of Psychology.

Iverson, G.L. and Lange, R.T. (2011). "Moderate and Severe Traumatic Brain Injury". Chapter 21 in M.R. Schoenberg and J.G. Scott (eds), *The Little Black Book of Neuropsychology: Syndrome-Based Approach* (pp. 663–696). New York, NY: Springer.

Jennett, B. and Teasdale, G.M. (1981). *Management of Head Injuries*. Philadelphia, PA: Davis.

Kinnunen, K.M., Greenwood, R., Powell, J.H., Leech, R., Hawkins, P.C., Bonnelle, V. and Sharp, D.J. (2010). "White matter damage and cognitive impairment after traumatic brain injury". *Brain*, 134(2), 449–463.

McCrea, M., Janecek, J.K., Powell, M.R. and Hammeke (2014). "Traumatic Brain Injury and the Postconcussion Syndrome". Chapter 10 in M.W. parsons and T.A. Hammeke (eds), *Clinical Neuropsychology: A Pocket Handbook for Assessment*, 3rd edition (pp. 208–236). Washington D.C.: American Psychological Association.

Ponsford, J., Sloan, S. and Snow, P. (1995). *Traumatic Brain Injury: Rehabilitation for Everyday Adaptive Living*. Hove: Lawrence Erlbaum Associates.

Roberts, C. (1994). "Post traumatic amnesia: shifting the focus of attention". In C. Haslam, J. Ewing, R. Farnbach, U. Johns and B.S. Weekes (eds), *Cognitive Functioning in Health, Disease and Disorder*. Sydney: Academic Press.

Shores, E.A. (1989). "Comparison of the Westmead PTA scale and the Glasgow Coma Scale as predictors of neuropsychological outcome following extremely severe blunt head injury". *Journal of Neurology, Neurosurgery and Psychiatry*, 52, 126–127.

Stambrook, M., Moore, A.D., Peter, L.C., Deviaenes, C. and Hawryluk, G.A. (1990). "Effects of mild, moderate and severe closed head injury on long-term vocational status". *Brain Injury*, 4(2), 183–190.

Symonds, C.P. and Russell, W.R. (1943). "Accidental head injuries: prognosis in service patients". *Lancet*, 1, 7–10.

Teasdale, G. and Jennett, B. (1974). "Assessment of coma and impaired consciousness: a practical scale". *The Lancet*, 2, 81–84.

Walsh, K.W. (1991). *Understanding Brain Damage: A Primer of Neuropsychological Evaluation*, 2nd edition. New York, NY: Churchill Livingstone.

Wilson, J.T., Teasdale, G.M., Hadley, D.M., Wiederman, K.D. and Lang, D. (1993). "Post-traumatic amnesia: still a valuable yardstick". *Journal of Neurology, Neurosurgery and Psychiatry*, 56, 198–201.

Chapter 3

Coma

Sheena and Allan: life before and after TBI

Many individuals played a part in resuscitating me and guiding my faltering progress. Prime amongst them must be Allan. He was then the BBC's Chief Correspondent in Moscow. In 1999, this was a relatively safe posting for a foreign correspondent accustomed to warzones, as he had been for many years, working in the Balkans, Africa and the Middle East, often in extreme and dangerous situations. The last place he expected to experience trauma was London.

We had met in the winter of 1993 at a conference at Wilton Park, the country retreat for the Foreign Office's think-tank, Chatham House: a couple of hundred NGO representatives and journalists were invited to spend four days talking about Western policy in the Balkans.

I looked at the programme. My contribution was on Tuesday, but on Sunday, there was a keynote speech by a name I recognised – the BBC foreign correspondent Allan Little. I had heard his radio broadcasts from Timişoara in Romania, then from Baghdad during the Gulf War, and most recently from Bosnia, and had thought he wrote and spoke well, and was clearly a very interesting thinker. Although I was working in London on Monday, I resolved to go to the conference twice, once to hear him, once to perform myself.

He talked about his recent experiences in Bosnia, and ended by saying, "This is what's happening, but of course you can't say that." I guessed why: because the BBC was following the official British government line at the time, and Allan – and I – felt it was wrong.

Allan offered to drive me back to London the following morning, and I accepted. When we parted, I had his phone number.

Some six months later, I called him and suggested that we meet for lunch so that he could share his Balkan expertise with me, although it turned out he knew no more than I did about the Bosnian Government's mindset.

"Do you fancy dinner in a couple of weeks?" he asked. Yes, I said. So we met again on the eve of my birthday. Two days later, Allan went back to work in Bosnia. He phoned me after a couple of days, and said those words every woman wants to hear: "Come to Sarajevo."

I had not been to Sarajevo since before the siege, back in the 1980s, when I had thought it one of the most vibrant and culturally fascinating places I had ever visited. Now, it was tragic – a fish-in-a-barrel shooting-range for Bosnian Serbs, where the citizens were obliged to live without water or electricity, surviving on occasional emergency food-parcels.

So how was I to go now? Apart from the logistical problems, I was presenting a weekly live international affairs TV programme in six days' time. But I felt sure that Channel 4 would sanction a co-presentation of *The World This Week* from Sarajevo. There were so many angles on what was happening there, and so many stories: for instance, I had met artists there, and an amazing man in charge of multiple art-forms, Miro Purivatra, who had been invited to take a show he had curated to the Venice Biennale and the Edinburgh Festival Fringe, but had not been able, in accord with United Nations policy, to leave his besieged city. I lobbied hard for the extra money we would need, and Channel 4 agreed to put up half the amount. Now all I needed was another £5,000 from the production company, Yorkshire Television. They refused, and I could not persuade them.

"Come to Sarajevo" rang in my ears.

I decided to go.

"But you've got to be back in time to present next week's pro-gramme," protested my producer.

I went, courtesy of a press pass issued by the UN peacekeeping force in Sarajevo: an overnight boat-ride, a Hercules C130 military aircraft (on which I was allowed into the cockpit as the pilot, carrying aid-parcels and sundry aid-workers, followed a near-vertical trajectory into the airport to avoid any flak from the besiegers) and finally an armoured personnel carrier which took civilians from the shattered airport into the smashed city. I arrived on Tuesday at the Holiday Inn in Sarajevo, where a multi-national community of journalists and photographers was staying. In the lobby I ran into a British photographer friend who said, "Miro's waiting for you," and immediately took me by a circuitous route to the art gallery where my Sarajevan friend was still working.

I met up with Allan at tea-time, and stayed in Sarajevo, with him, for four days. I made it back to London in time for the programme, and brought with me a film of defiant ongoing arts activity which I had shot with a local crew in Sarajevo (I had taken tape-stock and batteries in with me), and which I went on to sell to the BBC. I also smuggled out prints by the artists who were unable to send their work to the Edinburgh Festival, and these were framed and exhibited later that year.

And thus began the most important relationship of my life. Allan continued to work abroad, often in very dangerous places, but spent his time off and holidays with me.

So we had known each other for over five years. Most of that time we had spent living apart. A year before the injury, I had visited him in Moscow. I had floated the idea of some form of commitment. He said, "I guess I'm just an old bachelor. A moody, selfish old bachelor. Bear with me." I did.

Now he faced having to take care of someone whose long-term prospects were uncertain.

The hospital notes were unsentimental:

> CT scan showed a fracture of the right maxilla anteriorly extending into the orbital floor. An intracranial haemorrhage in the left occipital lobe was a small extra axial collection.

So the occipital lobe, the part of the brain that controls eyesight, had suffered a haemorrhage.

> She made some progress over the next 24 hours and following a repeat CT scan which showed resolution of the haematoma [a blood-clot within my skull], she was successfully extubated. She had also sustained a right pneumothorax which was drained.

In other words, fluid was building up in my chest – a pneumothorax – so I had a chest drain installed.

I had suffered a "closed" head injury. My skull was cracked above my right eye, and my cheek bone broken below it. I suffered internal cranial bleeding in the area that controls eyesight, and some blood-clotting, along with some internal chest damage, and a broken finger. My frontal lobe had been traumatised.

I say that this happened to me. Of course, it happened to my family, indirectly. The knock-on impact of any injury ripples out (see Figure 3.1). When I learned what my family had been through, watching me struggle up the long hill towards recovery, it was clear that they endured a different but equally disorienting process – and one which in some ways exceeded my own trauma.

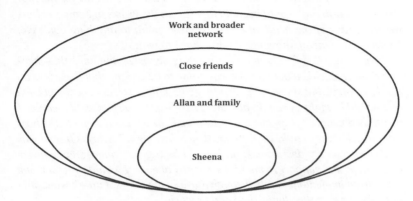

Figure 3.1 The pebble effect of a TBI as the impact ripples out from the individual

My younger sister Alison came down from Edinburgh on the following day, and remembers every newspaper reporting my injury, and my critical condition.

"I couldn't look at your face in the hospital. I focused on your lower legs and feet, which were unmarked. It was surreal.

"A bath next to your ward was filled to the brim with flowers from the likes of Tony and Cherie Blair, and Tim Rice. You weren't allowed them beside your bed – but you wouldn't have been aware anyway."

"I was rapidly learning the severity of the situation. 'The brain has the consistency of raw egg,' one of the doctors said.

"'Or think of a jelly in a dish being shaken around violently. Like every other organ in the body the brain swells up when it gets bruised. But because it's enclosed by the skull, the swelling has nowhere to expand to. That's why it's so dangerous. Sheena's brain is badly bruised and full of fluid that shouldn't be there. It has, consequently, ceased functioning. The normal tiny electrical impulses that constitute thought, cognitive process, even instinctive unconscious functions like breathing, have all shut down.'"

My bosses at the BBC had booked me into a hotel for a few days, around the corner from the hospital. In the early hours of the morning, after the nurse had tried to reassure me that he thought "this one's going to make it", I went and checked in and I'd fallen into a fitful sleep. Now I was back on the unit, early in the morning, and anxious to know more about what was happening.

"And when will those functions return?" I asked, and saw for the first time a reaction that would become familiar in the weeks to come: a blank neutral shake of the head and a refusal to commit to anything concrete. "There's no way of knowing. We just have to wait."

I sat by her bed for three days repeating my useless mantra that there had been an accident but that she was going to be alright, that there was no need to worry, that she was in hospital getting all the treatment she needed and would be right as rain in no time. There was no response. Sometimes I mentioned people I'd spoken to on the phone, or who had come to the hospital to see if they could visit. "I saw Chris last night" (Chris Greene was one of Sheena's oldest friends and would be a great, quiet, steady tower of strength and support to me in the months ahead). I wouldn't let anyone apart from immediate family through those swing doors. I didn't want anyone to see her in this diminished and precarious state.

I began to understand now how important the support of friends would become. I noticed that close friends reacted differently. Some didn't know what to say. Others didn't want to intrude and neither called nor visited. I came out through the swing doors of the Intensive Care Unit on the first day to find Peter Florence, the brilliant impresario who has built the Hay Festival into what it is today, standing by the lifts with a hamper of food. He was an old friend. I hugged him and found it hard to speak. Sarah Manwaring-White was one of Sheena's closest friends but I'd never met her. She too turned up at the swing doors. "If there's anything I can do please don't hesitate to ask," she said. "Actually there is," I said. "Can you go to Tesco for me?" It seemed such a mundane request but this is the kind of help you really do need. "Maybe get some bread, eggs, butter and milk so that Sheena's parents can at least have breakfast in the morning?" Sheena's parents were staying at her house in Islington. I expected Sarah to bring a small carrier bag back to the hospital from a shop around the corner. Instead, when Sheena's parents got home that night they found the fridge crammed with enough food to last a fortnight: Sarah hadn't stopped at milk and eggs; she'd also taken the trouble, without asking, to go to the house and stock the larder. Sarah also quietly arranged for a taxi to ferry Sheena's parents home every evening, sparing them what would otherwise have been, at their age, a tiring and difficult journey through an unfamiliar public transport system in one of the busiest capital cities in the world. These were thoughtful and kind things to do; they meant more to me than I could properly express.

I got myself a UK mobile phone. It rang off the hook. I kept it switched off in the hospital. Sometimes when I turned it on again there would be 30 new messages. There was simply no time even to listen to them, never mind reply. Often I deleted them without listening, otherwise I'd have spent hours every day responding to well-meaning and concerned friends, instead of being where I needed to be – with Sheena. I relied on a relatively small number of close friends – five or six – and asked them to spread the word whenever there was anything new to say.

On the second day, the Monday morning, I walked past a news stand and there, from the front page of the Daily Telegraph, Sheena's beautiful face, taken from a Channel 4 studio photo, shone out under a headline that said "TV Sheena" was in a "fight for life". I came to hate these military metaphors and their implication that there was some moral dimension to overcoming injury; that all you had to do was fight hard enough – as though success in the "fight" or the "battle" were contingent on your moral fibre and your determination to "win".

The newspapers rang every day and the ward nurses handled their calls with tact and courtesy, referring each call to the hospital media office, which simply repeated a short statement saying that Sheena's condition was "critical but stable". I had been keeping Sheena's closest friends away from her bedside – I thought they would be distressed by the sight of her and I hoped that one day Sheena would be grateful that I'd shielded her from view while her injuries were still so vivid and shocking. But a reporter from the Daily Mail very nearly got in. I stopped her at the swing doors. She had the decency to look abashed and didn't push when I asked her to leave. "It's my first day in this job," she said. I'm from that trade myself and knew how damaging it would be if she went back to her newsroom with nothing. I felt some sympathy for her but protecting Sheena was my priority.

Mostly for those first few days, the period of the coma, I sat by her bed and held her hand. Every few minutes I said "Squeeze my hand if you can hear me." There was not a flicker of a response. Sheena lay perfectly still, breathing to the rhythm of the ventilator that was keeping her alive. It seems odd now but I still hadn't given any real thought to the possibility that she might emerge from her coma with a condition that I was scared to name – irreparable brain damage. None of us allowed ourselves to think about the long-term; we were focused on the next step – waking from the coma – and no further. I would quickly learn that you seized on each tiny sign of an improvement and took heart from it and put out all thoughts about the long-term prospects.

Three days after the injury, there was still no response. The nurses began to prepare her for another brain scan.

I was still too new to all this, still too bewildered by it, that I had not yet learned to ask each medical professional who came to see Sheena who they were and what their job was. This was a mistake. A male medic, who I assumed must be a neurologist but probably wasn't and whose name I was never told (why didn't I ask him, politely, who he was?) said another scan would give some indication of the extent of the damage caused by some bleeding that had been observed at the back of the brain. Sheena had been hit on the front of the head; the area above the right eye had taken the force of the impact. But her brain had then ricocheted onto the back of the skull on the left side, in what the medics call a contracoup *(my new vocabulary was expanding). Boxers experience this and many suffer neurological consequences later in life, he said.*

This was a shocking moment. It was the first time the term "brain damage" had entered my thoughts. It conjured images of helplessness and incapacity that I didn't want to think about.

At around 11 a.m., the nurses wheeled the whole whirligig of life-support — bed, tubes, wires, screens flashing and beeping, monitors, ventilators — with Sheena lying insensible and silent at the heart of it, through the swing doors and out of sight. I sat by the empty space left by her bed for an hour. Then, suddenly, the whole thing reappeared and I heard the consultant talking to the nurses about "extubation".

This, someone explained, meant that they would disconnect the machinery of life support and try to make Sheena breathe again by herself.

Clearly things had started to move now but I was still preoccupied with the idea that had entered my head for the first time an hour earlier – the idea that there might be permanent brain damage. "It looks OK," the man I assumed to be the consultant neurologist said. "So we're going to try to take her off the ventilator today."

"But the bleeding, the brain haemorrhage you mentioned earlier, what about that?" I said. "Oh no, it's fine," he said casually, as though it were of trifling significance. "It's resolving itself."

I almost wept. I felt winded. Relief sweeps through you and you understand in that moment how tense and anxious you have been feeling. You will learn as the weeks go on that medical professionals do this every day. It is the air they breathe. They are not, cannot be, emotionally invested in it. They will do their job with great dedication and skill and determination, and you will be grateful to them, come to think of them as heroic, but they won't be remotely concerned about how you are feeling and will not tell you much UNLESS YOU ASK. I now understood that some of the injury Sheena's brain had incurred was healing. But it hadn't occurred to the consultant to tell me that until I ASKED.

That evening, 72 hours after the injury, Sheena began breathing unaided. Within a few hours she was starting to move. Then she was thrashing around, arms legs head, positioning and repositioning herself on the bed as though she were in the middle of some disturbed dream she couldn't escape from. It is a distressing sight, this; almost violent in its intensity, it looks as though the person you love is herself in great distress.

The nurses said it was a normal neurological response – her brain reestablishing contact with her limbs. "Her motor neurone responses seem to be in full working order anyway," said one of the nurses. It wasn't until that moment that I had confronted the knowledge that a brain injury, like a stroke, can paralyse the limbs.

And it was later that night that I got what I interpreted as my first response. "Sheena, please try for me. Squeeze my hand if you can hear me." I'd said it hundreds of times by now. And then, in the small hours of Tuesday morning, more than three days after the injury, I felt her fingers close and tighten a little around mine.

It was the first of those moments – the first tiny sign of progress – into which you invest so much hope. In that moment I had the overwhelming sensation – the certainty, even – that Sheena was in there somewhere, that my voice had registered with her, she had understood what that voice had said and had responded appropriately. I was wrong of course; the reaction could have meant anything or nothing. But you have to believe it, because hope is what keeps you going.

It hadn't occurred to me yet to consider the emotional and psychological toll all this was taking on me and on Sheena's family. That would come later – much later. But you have to be ready for it when it catches up with you.

It was the next day, four days after the injury, that Sheena opened her eyes for the first time and appeared to look around her. Not her eyes, in fact: one eye, the left. The right side of her face was still so badly swollen that the right eye remained closed. I saw that the whites of her eyes were a vivid crimson, and swollen so that her iris – Sheena has beautiful and distinctive green-blue eyes – appeared pressed into the damaged tissue of the eye ball, indented almost.

I think I expected her to register some distress at what she saw around her. Instead she was utterly impassive. Her right hand was elevated slightly in a sling to protect the broken finger. She looked at it with detachment and turned it round slowly, gazing at it as if wondering what it was. Then she closed her eye again and drifted off again. At least I knew now that she could see. Whatever the damage the occipital lobe had sustained, she wasn't going to be blind.

But it was the first indication I got that Sheena's cognitive functions had suffered devastating consequences. She appeared to have no interest at all in her own condition: no distress, no concern, no alarm, no curiosity.

Her frontal lobes had been injured so I looked up the word "lobotomy", a neurosurgical procedure that had been practised widely in the 1940s and 1950s but is now largely discredited. It derives from the Greek words lobos, *meaning lobes, and* tome, *meaning to cut or slice. Patients with psychotic disorders had their frontal lobes removed or disabled by the operation, just as Sheena's frontal lobes seemed to have been put out of action by the injury. I read that the operation often succeeded in removing psychotic symptoms but at a terrible cost: "reducing the complexity of psychic life", I learned, was one effect; mental activity was replaced by inertia and survivors were blunted in their emotional responses and restricted in intellectual range. Sheena was one of the most intellectually gifted and emotionally intelligent people I had ever known. I had to fight against the urge to imagine the worst: that those precious attributes, which defined her, made her what she was, might not come back. I decided early on not to walk that path and instead to seize on every small improvement – the squeezing of my hand, the opening of an eye, the evident retention of an ability to read – as a sign that things were moving in the right direction.*

Speech came next. The bruising to her face and torso had got angrier and more vivid in the days since the injury and I was worried that she was in pain, so asked her where it hurt. "Everywhere," she said. It was the first word since the injury. And then she said "My throat." This surprised me but I guessed that the forcing of thick tubes into a swollen windpipe and then, three days later, pulling those pipes out again must have had a bruising effect on the soft tissue in her throat.

I expected her to ask where she was and what had happened. She didn't – nor would she for many weeks. In these brief moments of wakefulness she just looked around her; impassive, incurious, unresponsive.

I suspect there is no one medical definition for "confusion", but I feel it was the right word for the state I was in. When I "came round" from the coma after three or four days, I am told I was very confused. Apparently, I recognised my parents, and brother and sister – my brother and his wife had been the first to see me, before any surgery was carried out – but not Allan.

After a few days, Sheena glanced up at the whiteboard behind the nurses' station. Her name had been written up there in red marker pen, her surname spelt with a Mac instead of a Mc. "They've misspelt my name," she said casually, as though that was the most grievous thing that had happened to her. "At least she can still read, as well as see," I thought. But she said nothing about being in a hospital bed; nothing about the immense machinery of life support that she was wired up to; nothing about the other patients in the unit or the uniformed nurses going about their business. Why wasn't she distressed about being in this cold and clinical and strange environment? Why wasn't she even curious enough to ask about it?

My mother was now staying at my house in Islington. She would get back every night around 9.30 p.m. to a telephone answering-machine full of messages. My sister-in-law Diane would spend the weekends in London to support my mother. She dealt with the messages. Sarah Manwaring-White – who had stocked the fridge – was another "life-line", my mother would tell me much later. "She waited at the hospital every night until I left, and we repaired to the pub for a drink and a smoke!" My mother had not touched a cigarette for many years. "She also arranged for a taxi to take me back. She had suggested this to her boss – instead of flowers. You had loads of flowers. Your doctors and nurses called it 'the shrine'."

My apparent progress was swiftly followed by a backwards step. Trauma followed trauma, as the hospital notes recorded, dispassionately:

> Following extubation, she remained confused but had no focal neurology. She was transferred to the plastics ward but unfortunately, due to her confusion, she fell out of bed and removed her chest drain and was therefore transferred back to the Intensive Care Unit for closer observation.

This factual description of my fifth night in hospital misses out crucial detail: that I had been transferred from the Intensive Care Unit to a private room.

I don't remember now how the decision to move Sheena was taken or by whom but I understood that there was a desire to get her out of intensive care, now that she was conscious and breathing by herself, partly to make room for other patients whose hold on life was more precarious than Sheena's had become. It seems absurd now but my main concern was that she might be put in a room with a mirror and would catch sight of herself for the first time and that this would cause her huge distress. It irritated me slightly that the medical staff with whom I raised this didn't seem to share my concern or, indeed, even take it seriously. *As with much of what I experienced in the intensity of those first days, the reason for their nonchalance would become clear to me only when I thought about it in retrospect: for I would learn in the days ahead what they already knew only too well but did not communicate to me – that the part of Sheena's brain that was responsible for responding with distress was simply not functioning; that she was, for now, cognitively incapable of experiencing distress or anxiety or fear or worry even if she did catch sight of herself in a mirror.*

Anxiety is a universal attribute and not only among human beings: even the cattle in the fields around the house I grew up in experienced anxiety when something spooked them; but actual worry? I began to think of this as a very advanced and probably uniquely human function, the product of a very highly evolved brain, and wondered whether Sheena would ever again acquire the ability – the talent – to worry. It turns you upside down, this experience: who would have thought that I would ever yearn for the ability to feel worried?

I asked to see the room Sheena was to be moved to. What was I thinking? That if I didn't like it, I could somehow veto the move and keep her in intensive care till something better came up? It didn't occur to me that she would try to get out of bed when she was clearly so badly injured. I still hadn't grasped the simple fact that is central to the early stages of brain injury recovery: that the patient has absolutely no insight into her new condition; no idea that she is injured at all. "I think we should go home now," she had said several times, oblivious to the fact that she was attached by wires and tubes to so much gadgetry. "No point in staying here." It didn't occur to me that she would actively try to go home under her own steam. But why wouldn't she? She didn't know she was in hospital, didn't know she had been run over by a police van. I had told her repeatedly this was the case but her brain wasn't laying down new memories. She would take it in at the time, but in a moment or two the knowledge was gone again. "We should be getting home now. No point in staying here."

Sheena, despite being an NHS patient, was moved into a room in a part of the hospital normally reserved for private patients. It was a single room. I was glad of the privacy. I had no idea how dangerous that privacy would be.

The phone in my hotel room rang at around 5 in the morning. There was a voice on the other end that sounded nervous, as though he was about to break some bad news. He sounded contrite too. Something had gone wrong that revealed the foolishness of leaving Sheena without the constant attention that was normal in the Intensive Care Unit. Sheena

*had decided to get up and out of bed, and had instantly fallen over. Had
she banged her head again it could easily have been fatal. The doctor on
the other end of the line was right to be contrite. Somebody had made a
bad decision and the result could have been disastrous.*

*I didn't have the heart to feel angry. I had been very taken with
the extraordinary skill and dedication of the medical staff caring for
Sheena. Mostly what I felt was relief that she was OK and back in
the Intensive Care Unit. I got dressed and went into the unit to begin
another long day by her bedside trying to understand what was happening and to grapple with the long-term consequences, still not yet
fully understanding the central reality – that nothing would be the same
again; that there would eventually emerge a new normal. It takes a
long time to grasp this.*

As I understand it, the nurse looking after me did not understand or was
not told that I required constant round-the-clock monitoring, so left the
room. I was unable to stand or even sit – and yet had tried to leave the
bed – and, of course, fallen on the floor, wrenching out all my life-support
tubes. This could have been very serious. The conventional wisdom is
that if there is another "accident" within a week or two of the first one,
there may be a reaction which is disproportionately severe. Massive and
sometimes fatal brain swelling can occur.

When my mother was told the following morning, she says she was
incandescent with fury.

"We had visited the private ward you were taken to on your first day
there. A young nurse, with limited English, was sitting beside you and
tried to give you a drink. I pointed out that you would choke, and she
desisted.

"The next day around 5 a.m. I was phoned by the hospital. They said
you had got out of bed, thus disconnecting all the pipes attached to you.
I got to the hospital early and asked to see the consultant. I told him I
was very worried about this incident, and he replied, 'Not as worried as
I was.'"

Back to the Intensive Care Unit I went. In all, I was to spend two
weeks in intensive care, now being constantly monitored.

*The emotional numbness caused by the injury to the frontal lobes of her
brain was disguised to begin with by the fact that she was drifting in and
out of wakefulness. Gradually she began to speak whole sentences. But
they didn't make any sense. Grammatically they were fine, in the sense
that the parts of speech were all in the right order and in a coherent*

relationship with each other. It was just that the content was meaning-less. *It was as though a noun had been selected at random and dropped into the place in the sentence where the noun belonged, and the same with every other word. I wrote one of the exchanges into my diary, and I still have it. It went like this:*

Sheena: My plates are coming tomorrow.
Me: Plates? What plates?
Sheena: So does that mean you can't yet . . . [long pause] . . . speak in forecasts?
Me: No.
Sheena: [very surprised] How amazing!

A long pause followed.

Sheena: I get to present my comfort tomorrow.
Me: What's that?
Sheena: I'd like to go home soon.
Me: We will go home soon.
Sheena: That's like the statue.
Me: What statue?
Sheena: You know – like the holy animal.
Me: What, you mean like a cow?
Sheena: Could be a cow. Or a kitten. Or a hen.

When she started a sentence, it was as though her brain would decide for itself what she was trying to say and then come out with utter nonsense – names of people, places and things would be replaced with close but completely meaningless alternatives or replacement-words.

For days she drifted in and out, talking like this, each day getting a little stronger. Her periods of wakefulness grew more frequent and each lasted a little longer. Each time I told her about the accident it was as though she was hearing it for the first time, and seemed surprised and, eventually, a little bit alarmed. I was glad of this. The gradual recovery of a capacity to show alarm, however slight and however brief, seemed to me a sign that some cognitive function was returning. I think it is natural to do this, to seize on small moments and invest them with great significance. It is a far healthier and more constructive thing to do than to let imagination lead you into some bleak prognosis of hopelessness. In the early weeks of her recovery Sheena was surrounded by patients who were moving in the opposite direction. Many of them had neuro-degenerative conditions and were getting worse. Sheena, at least, seemed, by tiny increments, to be improving.

*After a week in this state, drifting in and out, talking nonsense, making
no sense, Sheena was still in intensive care, still unable to eat, still quite
unaware of where she was and what had happened.*

"Do you know where we are?" I asked.

*"Of course," she said. "In White City." White City was a BBC build-
ing in West London where we had both worked on current affairs projects.*

*I joked with friends that she had seen a cold and impersonal environment
full of incomprehensible and alienating machinery, in an atmosphere of
casual disregard, and had of course – why wouldn't you? – mistaken it
for a BBC workplace.*

*A week after the injury she was due to have surgery on her face, to
reset the bones that had been broken from her eye socket, down through
her right cheek bone and upper jaw. She would have to have an L-shaped
titanium pin screwed into the bone beneath her right eye.*

*I rehearsed in my head how I would break the news to her, because,
naturally, I thought the prospect of facial surgery would be alarming to
her. Sheena made her living on television and although she wasn't vain,
her appearance mattered to her. I still hadn't grasped the emotionally
numbing effect of the frontal lobe injury; still hadn't grasped that to feel
alarm was something beyond her cognitive ability.*

*When I did tell her, she seemed unmoved by it, utterly passive and
said simply "When?"*

"On Friday afternoon," I said.

*This emotional numbing would become familiar to me. It was a func-
tion of the injury and would, in the weeks ahead, recede as the swelling
in her brain went down.*

*She appeared to think for a moment and then said, dismissively,
"Seems unnecessary to me." Then a pause, and then: "Let's just go
home then and come back in for that."*

I kept referring to Allan as John – the name of a childhood boyfriend
who has lived with his wife and family in Sydney for years. Confused
minds play trick after trick.

The major facial operation took place a week after the injury. Initially,
the surgeons thought they would have to peel back my face, and enter via
my eye socket. In fact, they were able to do all the work via my mouth.
My dentist tells me I now have an impressive scar inside my mouth.

Channel 4 Television sent the surgeons the latest press photographs
they had of me, ironically taken in a hospital, so that my face could
be reconstructed as accurately as possible. Formally, the hospital notes
recorded what was done:

The zygomatic fracture was elevated and reduced via an intra-oral approach and fixed with one plate to the zygomatic buttress on 5 March. All healed well, and the associated intra-orbital nerve paraesthesia improved.

My mother reports that the young surgeon had come back into the ward, and said it had gone well. "In a year's time, you won't be able to tell," he said. Actually, you could still tell. There was a scar, and a dip, and a bump. But he did a good job, I think.

Months later, one of my consultants asked me if I had considered cosmetic surgery. Not yet, I replied – but then I had lost the habit of looking in mirrors.

It took far longer to operate on my oblique finger-fracture. That finger forever remains bent and swollen, and contains two titanium pins. I can never wear rings on it again. I also have an L-shaped titanium pin in my cheek. For the rest of my life, there will be tender spots on my face.

It was around this time that I began to get the impression for the first time that she didn't really know who I was. I was scribbling things down in a little pocket notebook. This is what I wrote now:

Somewhere in the space her head encloses is Sheena. I miss her. Where is she? Can she find her way back out? I'm so scared that this bizarre behaviour will not go away, that she'll live for ever now in this scrambled world that mixes past and present at random, that resurrects long-forgotten people and experiences and transplants them to the present and then just as quickly forgets and moves on.

That day she'd asked after her grandmother, who'd been dead for 15 years. Gradually I realised that Sheena's memory was shot away. The neurologists call this post-traumatic amnesia (see Figure 2.2). It has two aspects. The first and most obvious is retrograde amnesia – the apparent wiping-out of years of memory before the injury. Sheena seemed to have lost about 15 years. The second is short-term or antero-grade amnesia – the inability to remember new experiences, to lay down new memories. Sheena couldn't remember what happened five minutes ago, an hour ago. She had no concept of time passing – no knowledge of what day it was, what time of day it was, no knowledge of even which month or year it was. There was no past and no future, just a never-ending present, a permanent now. One day her father left her bedside to go out for a walk. When he returned an hour later she greeted him as though she hadn't seen him for months and said she was "amazed" to see him so unexpectedly. I had been at her bedside all morning, three or four hours. A nurse came to take her to the bathroom. On the way back the nurse asked whether she'd had any visitors that day. "No. No-one at all," she said.

After two weeks in intensive care, the medical notes document my still-fragile condition:

> She underwent manipulation of her finger fracture on the 5 March and she also had a repeat chest drain inserted at that stage. Following these procedures she remained very confused and cerebrally irritable but continued to have normal focal neurology. Her confusion failed to resolve over the next few days and she was transferred to the National Hospital for Neurology and Neurosurgery for ongoing head injury management.

This is a dry precis of developments. Allan reckons he initiated the transfer. He later told me that he became increasingly concerned because although my temperature, urine and blood were being regularly tested, no-one seemed to be assessing the full picture. He insisted on being given some kind of progress report, and the decision was thereafter made to send me to another hospital. No-one can spend a long time in intensive care. The beds are precious and sought-after.

I was learning something else too: that nobody will tell you anything unless you ask. Sheena was being seen regularly by many specialists who passed through the Intensive Care Unit. A consultant came to look at her eyes. Her blood pressure was checked every hour, there was a machine to measure the oxygen content of the blood, the output from her bladder, a saline drip to keep her hydrated. There were regular visits from a physiotherapist to assess whether there had been any damage to her motor functions (they thought not but couldn't be sure). The fluid on her lung was monitored. And with each specialist who came to tend her I would ask the same questions: why is she making no sense? Why doesn't she know where she is? Will this confusion, this fog, ever lift? And time after time I got the same answer: sorry, that's not my field.
To begin with I was scrupulously polite and instinctively deferential to a caste of people, the medics, whom I admired and held in great esteem, and to whom after all I had every reason to be grateful. But as Sheena's "dreamtalk", as I called it, persisted, my anxiety deepened and

eventually, confronted again with the same answer – Sorry, not my field – I said in some exasperation: "Then I want to talk to someone whose field it is! Whose field is it and why, when clearly this is the most obvious thing that is now wrong with her, is the only person not to have visited her the person whose field it is?"

I was learning to be assertive. I don't think I was ever discourteous and I have always disliked those who behave with an inflated sense of entitlement. But I came to understand how much depends on a willingness to challenge, in an articulate, confident and intelligent way, decisions that were being made but not communicated properly to me or Sheena's family. I began to see how important it was to be taken seriously by the medical professionals, whose instinct, in an often frantic work schedule, was to administer the treatment to the highest standard and then to take it for granted that the families of the patient would be content with what had been done. I was not content. I began to think that Sheena was not getting the attention she most needed.

Becoming more assertive seemed to change things. The consultant in charge of intensive care, whom I had never met, came to see me. He explained that the specialist Sheena now needed most was a neurologist. Of course that now seems obvious, laughably so. But this was the great lesson I was now learning – nobody tells you anything; you have to ask; and you have to not worry how daft medical professionals might think your questions are.

The question was – which neurologist? The Intensive Care Unit wanted Sheena out; there was nothing more they could do for her. It went on for days. "It's the politics of beds," a nurse said, cryptically. They were looking for somewhere to send her. Someone said the obvious place was the Oliver Zangwell Centre in Ely in Cambridgeshire, which specialised in brain injury rehabilitation. I began to think about how I would cope with this. I would rent a house and buy a car and stay there while Sheena was being treated, I decided; I couldn't really afford to do either.

Finally we were told that a bed was available at the National Hospital for Neurology and Neurosurgery at Queen Square in London. "Queen Square", as it's commonly known, was a UK centre of excellence: patients with difficult conditions not readily treatable at their local General Hospital would be referred to Queen Square. This was difficult for relatives who would often have to make long journeys from their home towns across the UK and incur the costs of travel and overnight accommodation to visit. But for us it was a stroke of good fortune; we had a home in London.

I told Sheena we were moving. She didn't show much interest. Then hospital orderlies came and began to wheel Sheena away. I watched her sitting upright in her hospital bed with a plaid blanket around her shoulders, suddenly disoriented. "I'll see you there!" I said. "Where? Where? I don't know where to meet you. . ." she called out, still unaware that she was being looked after in a hospital and would be taken care of. But again that "Where? Where?" cheered me. It was a question, after all, and suggested an awakening curiosity, something she had initiated, and that, in turn, told me that two weeks after the injury she was at least now cognitively capable of knowing that there was something she didn't know and perhaps needed to. These are the small signs of progress to which you cling.

Chapter 4

Trauma

I was transferred to the John Young Ward of the National Hospital for Neurology and Neurosurgery in Queen Square in central London on 11 March 1999, for ongoing head-injury management.

The National is a UK centre of excellence in the NHS. It is highly over-subscribed, and full of patients whose families must travel to London if they want to see them. It has a direct relationship with University College Hospital's Intensive Care Unit where I had spent two weeks. I was still suffering from post-traumatic amnesia (PTA).

Any traumatic brain injury causes multiple changes – physical, cognitive, behavioural, social and emotional. For instance, I remained reliant on a catheter. Blood became a normal part of life. My medical notes reveal that my right ear was full of blood. I had daily nose-bleeds, and for months blood crusted inside my nostril. I had a tube going into my chest, under my arm. And I was nursed through my monthly period.

I was losing weight. I had not eaten throughout my weeks at University College Hospital. The National's speech therapist, Trish Gilpin, noted that my swallow had not been assessed, so she tried out teaspoons of water and ice-cream on me, and recorded that "laryngeal movement is poor, and non-existent on ice-cream." My brain had forgotten how to swallow. Even on water, I coughed. Trish recommended that I should be, for the moment, a nil-by-mouth patient, although she recognised that having had some nasal surgery, it would be hard to pass a nasogastric (NG) liquid-feeding tube into me. She also recognised that I was getting hungry.

Despite Trish Gilpin's fears, a tube was effectively inserted, under the supervision of a man who had seen me at UCH, to where he had been called because my intubation there was difficult.

Stages of recovery: from intensive care to acute neurorehabilitation

Sheena was admitted to the National Hospital under the care of Dr. Richard Greenwood, Consultant Neurologist and rehabilitation physician. Following a TBI, "waking up" or emerging from a loss of consciousness can be slow or rapid or anything in between. Once admitted to A&E, urgent medical issues are treated and then patients are closely monitored in an Intensive Care Unit. Sheena spent about two weeks being closely monitored at this stage before she was transferred to the National Hospital for acute neurorehabilitation (see Figure 4.1). The overarching principle in the acute stage is to implement any form of neurorehabilitation concurrent with ongoing medical treatment. This also means that acute cognitive status can be affected by physical factors such as hydration, nutrition, pain, oxygen needs, and infection, to name a few.

At the time of transfer, Sheena was confused and irritable. It is not uncommon for TBI patients to experience both PTA and agitation at this transitional or "in between" stage. As alertness and arousal increases, before brain functions are restored, cognition and behaviour can be very confused and misdirected.

Dreamtalk: *what lies between coma and consciousness*

Dreamtalk. What an apt term for the state "in-between" unconsciousness and consciousness. I was struck by this term when Allan said this was his word for

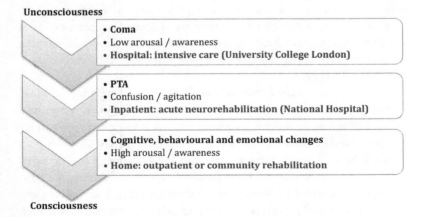

Figure 4.1 Stages of recovery and neurorehabilitation

the nonsensical conversations that he frequently had with Sheena. Yes, there is retrieval of information but there is a lack of coherence and minimal (if any) checking or monitoring of whether the information is relevant or makes sense in itself, given the question asked or topic of conversation. In many ways, this is what is meant by "socially-appropriate behaviour given the context". At this in-between stage of PTA, Sheena is not socially appropriate. The clear distinction in cognition is that Sheena's *automatic* processes are starting to engage but her conscious or *voluntary control* of these processes are not. In other words, the parts of her brain that process information are starting to work but the frontal lobes that control our cognition and behaviour, and enable us to be relevant, are not yet engaged. I will briefly overview the functions of the frontal lobe here as they help understand Sheena's *dreamtalk*.

Understanding frontal lobe functions

Classical theories of brain function broadly propose an anterior/posterior division of roles, like that put forth by the Russian neurologist Alexander Luria, which is neatly translated and summarised in *The Working Brain* (Luria, 1973). In the last 40 years, frontal lobe functions have been further refined by individuals like Tim Shallice, whom I have been fortunate enough to work with, and his colleagues including Don Stuss, amongst others. In fact, before I moved to London in 1996, my first clinical neuropsychology supervisor in Australia and I discussed Tim's landmark paper in *Brain* (Shallice and Burgess, 1991). We were struck by the detailed case studies of patients with frontal lobe damage who had very high levels of intelligence alongside "executive" deficits that meant that they had difficulty with practical tasks like shopping. This fascinated me and sowed the seeds for my orientation towards frontal lobe functions (and my later work with Tim) well before I met Sheena in 1999.

Whilst there are many frameworks for frontal lobe function and cognitive control (e.g., see reviews by Badre, 2008, and Diamond, 2013), it is the work of Tim and colleagues that has influenced my own thinking and approach to neurorehabilitation with individuals like Sheena over the last 20 years. Put simply, it helps understand the specialisation and functions of specific parts of the frontal lobe, in relation to the posterior regions of the brain, and how this impacts thinking and behaviour. In a brief review paper, Stuss (2011) summarised four sets of processes that work together for voluntary control of behaviour, as follows:

1   *Energization* or sustained activation, which is necessary in order to produce any response in the absence of input.

2   *Executive processes* that identify what is required to complete a task and then sets the rules in place (*task setting*), followed by *monitoring* to check behaviour is appropriate.

3   *Emotional and behavioural regulation* integrates the motivational, reward/risk, emotional and social aspects of behaviour with responses, given the external context.

4   *Integrative or meta-cognitive function* is the reflective aspect to see if what is occurring is appropriate and, if not, adjust to accomplish complex novel behaviours.

As a patient emerges or wakes up from a coma, the process of *energization* starts to operate and drive responding; this makes it possible for Sheena to be awake, aroused and then to produce a response without input such as a question or picture prompt. At this point her *executive processes* are operating minimally, if at all. I mean that she may produce a response but there is no *task setting* to ask what is required or evaluation of a response with respect to what was asked; that is, no *monitoring* to check what she said was appropriate or meaningful to the context. *Behavioural and emotional regulation* are not even on the horizon at this point, let alone thinking about one's thinking – aka *meta-cognition*!

Acute environmental management

Before a patient can voluntarily and actively engage in their own treatment and rehabilitation, *passive environmental management* strategies can be helpful and are often pivotal in navigating this in-between stage. This approach is for patients in PTA and/or presenting with agitation. These are simple strategies implemented on the ward that aim to reduce confusion and increase orientation, which will result in an indirect modification of behaviour. This is adopted when it is not possible for a patient to participate. When a patient is able to participate, even if in a limited manner, *active behaviour modification* techniques can be used, which will result in a direct modification of behaviour. These depend on associational learning that is impaired in coma-emerging patients or those in PTA.

In the Acute Brain Injury Unit at the National Hospital, we devised a formal protocol in 2005 to manage patients that were confused and/or agitated with environmental strategies adopted first, and medication as a second line of management. This approach aims to avoid sedating a patient whose brain is "waking up" and regaining function, whenever possible. We developed three simple principles, with specific actions, which were available as posters to place at bedside as a reminder for staff and family. In essence these are the three principles of *environmental management*:

1 Reduce the level of stimulation in the environment:

- avoid overstimulation and visual distraction
- monitor room temperature for comfort
- room should be in area of low traffic but able to be monitored easily
- limit visitors and orient visitors regarding strategies
- during therapies, eliminate or reduce activities that cause annoyance, frustration and overstimulation
- avoid excessive touching and handling.

2 Reduce the patient's confusion:

- provide consistent staffing
- avoid moving rooms
- allow one person to speak at a time
- communicate clearly and concisely (i.e. one idea at a time)
- keep a consistent schedule for therapies and activities (i.e. routine)
- re-orient to place, time, and purpose through the day
- keep area well-lit during day and dark and quiet at night
- promote sleep.

3 Tolerate restlessness and agitation as much as possible:

- review with staff specific strategies to be used for each patient and "crisis intervention" techniques
- allow patient to thrash about on the floor or in bed
- allow mobile patient to pace around the unit, supervised
- allow confused patient to be verbally inappropriate.

For Sheena, these principles were applied, albeit informally, once she was transferred to the National Hospital. When I look back, Allan and Sheena's parents would have found this useful in the two weeks prior to transfer when Sheena was in the Intensive Care Unit and also whilst Sheena was still in PTA at the National Hospital.

Acute neurorehabilitation: the multidisciplinary team

The overarching goal of neurorehabilitation is to maximise the optimal level of function and facilitate recovery by attaining skills that reduce the impact of the brain injury on everyday functioning. Outcomes are generally better when there is an organised *multidisciplinary team*, including speech, physical and occupational therapists, and neuropsychologists (Guy *et al.*, 2004). The role of a *physiotherapist* is to assist with improving motor function (e.g., strength, co-ordination, sitting, walking). An *occupational therapist* will focus on functional independence through activities like dressing and washing, then later cooking and shopping; they can assist with practical modifications to facilitate independence. A *speech therapist* can assist with physical speech difficulties including feeding and the co-ordination of swallow, as well as broader language problems (e.g., verbal expression and understanding speech). Soon after admission, for example, Sheena was referred to speech therapist Trish Gilpin for assessment of her capacity to swallow. At this time Sheena remained nil by mouth and she was unable to eat or drink, which affects hydration and nutrition status. Also part of a multidisciplinary team are nurses experienced with neurological conditions who regularly monitor medical and neurological status. A *clinical neuropsychologist* assesses, monitors and manages disorders related to *cognition, mood and behaviour*. In simple terms, these brain functions can be disturbed when there is an injury or damage. For instance, following a TBI a patient may present with a disturbance to one or more cognitive functions (e.g., memory, attention, language, visual perception). At the acute stage, assessment of cognitive status and ability can help determine an individual's capacity to engage in other types of therapy and inform rehabilitation goals.

A series of tests was carried out to assess my cognitive functions. I was initially examined by consultant neurologist Dr. Richard Greenwood, who recommended that clinical neuropsychologist Gail Robinson see me. This was the beginning of what would become a vital and long-term relationship with Gail. The day after I arrived at the National, she assessed me. Since I had no idea that anything was happening, I could not fake my responses, or try to create a good impression. Gail had never met me, and knew nothing of me. Some years later, I read her first report:

> Verbal subtest scores were all borderline defective except for Digit Span which was low average . . . Her reading performance . . . gives an estimated premorbid optimal level of functioning in the superior

range (Reading IQ equivalent 120). Her current performance on test of general intelligence, therefore, reflects a severe degree of intellectual under-functioning.

Her memory functions are impaired. She is still in a state of post-traumatic amnesia in which she is unable to lay down and consolidate daily memories. On a very easy verbal recognition test her memory was poor . . . Upon questioning there was evidence of retrograde amnesia as she is unable to recall events prior to the accident, e.g., special holidays from 1998, details about her last job.

There was evidence for a severe nominal dysphasia. She was given a formal test of word retrieval – a test for a condition called expressive aphasia. This assesses the recall of ordinary vocabulary. Sheena was shown simple pictures of everyday objects – cup, house, dog, car – and was asked to name them. She obtained a very impaired score (3/30). However, she had no difficulty understanding test instructions. Verbal IQ of 75.

A verbal IQ of 75 is subnormal. Was I destined to be intellectually impaired for the rest of my life?

I had experienced significant "frontal lobe dysfunction", and my performance on a simple test of speed and attention was "both slow and inefficient". All in all, Gail Robinson concluded that I was currently functioning "in the borderline scale on the verbal range".

Clinical neuropsychology

Sheena was referred to me due to her continuing confusion and disorientation. At the time I received the referral, I did not absolutely know the name "Sheena McDonald" although there was a vague familiarity. My first impression when I walked onto the John Young ward, however, was that this was a very popular person! It was full of visitors and numerous colourful bouquets at the nurses' station; there was a kind of *buzz*. But this busy setting was the exact opposite of what I needed in order to accurately assess the cognitive status of a TBI patient at bedside!

I pulled the curtain for privacy and began my questioning of this courteous but confused patient with an intense gaze. Sheena struck me as highly intelligent with extremely well-articulated, even if nonsensical, speech. The bedside neuropsychology assessment was short and limited, due to the ward environment and the fact that Sheena was only able to concentrate for a very short time. These factors affect test choice and comprehensiveness of an assessment.

Neuropsychological assessment

What is a neuropsychological assessment and what does it tell us? It can answer questions about whether a person has cognitive impairment and, if so, what is the nature and extent of this. In some instances we can determine if the cognitive impairment is due to organic brain factors, or if there might be another cause; in Sheena's case, there was no doubt about the cause. The aftermath of the TBI was hard to miss. To answer questions about cognitive status, a clinical neuropsychologist conducts an assessment to (1) estimate the pre-TBI level of functioning and (2) measure current post-TBI level of functioning. How do we estimate an individual's premorbid ability? This is done either by the reading method or by considering other factors such as educational background and occupational experience, or by using a combination of both (for detailed explanations see Cipolotti and Warrington, 1995; Lezak, Howieson, Loring and Fischer, 2004). In Sheena's case both clearly placed her well above an average person; in fact, her performance on a standard reading test (National Adult Reading Test, Nelson and Willison, 1991) estimated her premorbid intelligence level to be within the superior range (NART IQ 120; see Table 4.1). This was corroborated by her educational background (Honours degree from Edinburgh University) and her occupational experience, which I quickly learned to be vast and unusual!

To assess the current level of cognitive functioning, an analytic procedure that is like an experiment with the guiding conceptual framework being one of hypothesis testing, is undertaken. A full neuropsychological assessment would include an investigation of general intelligence, memory, spoken and written language, visual perception, praxis, higher order "executive" functions, attention, and speed of processing (see what follows for an overview). It involves measuring the current level of cognitive function using a series of tests that are reliable (i.e., they have been shown to produce the same result over time) and valid (i.e., they have been shown to measure what they are designed to measure). The premorbid and current levels of cognitive functioning are then compared in order to ascertain whether cognitive impairments are present. A cognitive profile can be constructed that compares scores across all of the cognitive domains assessed with the results becoming part of the picture. In addition, qualitative aspects of an individual's behaviour during an assessment contribute to a full profile of the current level of functioning. Assessment of mood includes information from observation, interview, and it may also include formal self-report measures (e.g., "The hospital anxiety and depression scale", Zigmond and Snaith, 1983), but not when a patient remains confused like Sheena was at this point. All of this information taken together informs and guides the next step in terms of immediate interventions, ongoing management and further rehabilitation needs.

Cognitive domains and disorders: overview

- General intelligence: the set of mental skills that enable an individual to perceive and understand the world, to reason and solve problems, and to adapt behaviour for the environment. A further division can be made with crystallised intelligence referring to acquired knowledge about the world and fluid intelligence referring to the ability to reason and solve novel problems. This is assessed by intelligence scales that comprise many subtests that tap verbal comprehension, perceptual reasoning, working memory and processing speed (e.g., Wechsler Adult Intelligence Scale) or nonverbal abstract reasoning tasks (e.g., Raven's Advanced Progressive Matrices). An individual may be compromised in some subtests or in all aspects, showing global intellectual decline.

- Memory and amnesia: disorders of memory can affect personal memories (autobiographical memory), learning new information (episodic memory) or general knowledge about the world (semantic memory). Amnesia can occur for verbal or visual information (selective amnesia) or both (global amnesia). As detailed previously, PTA is specific to the memory disturbance that follows a TBI. In addition, loss of previously stored memories is retrograde amnesia and the inability to learn new information is known as anterograde amnesia; both can be impaired once PTA is no longer present, following a TBI.

- Language and aphasia: language disorders can affect speaking (expressive aphasia) or understanding (receptive aphasia) or both (global aphasia). The most common language disorder affects the ability to retrieve words or names of objects, people or places (nominal aphasia). At the early message generation stage of language, an individual may have difficulty thinking of what they want to say (dynamic aphasia). I will discuss these further, in relation to Sheena.

- Literacy and numeracy: dyslexia is the term used when the problem is with reading; dysgraphia refers to spelling problems; and dyscalculia is when arithmetic difficulties are present. Problems with any of these skills can arise after a TBI.

- Perception and agnosia: disorders: of perception (or agnosia) can occur in any of the five senses (touch, taste, hearing, smell and vision). The most commonly assessed is vision. First, is visual information arriving via the optic nerves to the visual (occipital) cortex? That is, early visual processes are assessed (acuity, colour, movement, shape, location). If these "early" visual processes are intact, do you recognise what you are looking at (visual perception) and do you know exactly where something is in the surrounding environment (visuospatial perception)? Sheena had primary damage to the face area surrounding the right eye as well as persistent diplopia, or double vision. By contrast, her early visual processes and ability to recognise and localise objects was well-preserved.

- Movement and apraxia: difficulties in the ability to move your hands or mouth when asked can manifest as apraxia. For example, limb apraxia is when you are unable to execute actions with the limbs (e.g., waving or brushing your teeth) and buccofacial apraxia is when you have difficulty making movements with your mouth (e.g., coughing or sipping through a straw).

- Frontal "executive" functions: these are the abilities that enable an individual to adapt their behaviour in order to respond and interact appropriately in any situation (see previous for detail). There are many functions that come under this umbrella term in a multidisciplinary neurorehabilitation team including decision-making, planning, organisation, reasoning, abstraction, flexibility, shifting, self-regulation, inhibition, initiation, judgement, monitoring, strategic thinking and so on. Broadly, these are the processes that enable complex behaviours, hence the term "high-level" functions. These skills can be disturbed separately or several of these skills may be affected. Clinical neuropsychologists often use the analogy that the executive functions are the Chief Executive Officer (or CEO) of the brain, or that these abilities are akin to being the conductor of the symphony. These abilities are frequently affected for a long time after a TBI, in pronounced or subtle forms. I will discuss specific skills shortly.

- Attention and concentration: disorders of attention and concentration are common after any TBI. Selective or focusing attention, sustaining attention over time or dividing attention between tasks are all aspects of attention that can be altered. These skills are crucial for frontal lobe functions, which have also been termed the "Supervisory Attentional System" (e.g., Norman and Shallice, 1986; Stuss, 2011). It is rare that attention and concentration remain intact when an individual is in a state of PTA; fundamentally, these and memory are the core abilities impacted during PTA.

- Speed of processing: when information processing is disturbed, thinking can be slowed down and other cognitive skills can be affected and manifest as inefficiencies, as the amount of information processed may be limited.

Sheena's bedside neuropsychology assessment

After my first meeting with Sheena, who was still in a state of PTA after two weeks, I was extremely cautious about long-term prognosis. At this time, I knew that PTA duration of longer than a few days was not good, yet I also knew that there was much debate about how to measure PTA and how to distinguish between a temporary state of confusion and longer-term memory impairment. For instance, when does PTA end and continuous memory resume? This is hard to unequivocally measure and later my colleagues (Baird et al., 2005) demonstrated that identifying the moment when one is "out of PTA" is somewhat arbitrary; this study showed that about 50% of patients no longer in a state of PTA, as measured by our PTA tests, in fact had significant memory impairments on formal tests!

Sheena's results were brief and largely indicative of very impaired cognitive abilities. At the acute stage, I am often searching for islands of "preservation". After a severe TBI this can be akin to searching for a needle in a haystack. For Sheena, automatic and overlearned skills like reading and visual perception were well-preserved (see Table 4.1). The latter was despite damage to her right eye and the vision area of the brain (the occipital lobe). I was not surprised by these two cognitive skills being preserved even though Sheena was still confused, as these skills are associated with posterior regions of the brain; the left and right temporal lobes, respectively. A third area that did surprise me and cause me to hope was Sheena's average performance on the Raven's Advanced Progressive Matrices test of fluid intelligence. This test requires higher reason and novel problem-solving; it is related to adaptive abilities and frontal "executive" functions. These three islands of "relative" preservation were important flags for me to leave room for change in my conclusions.

In our written reports, clinical neuropsychologists use terms like "impairment", "deficit" and "reduction"; there is no satisfactory way to convey cognitive dysfunction and brain damage! I used the term "underfunction" for Sheena, which implies that performance is currently very poor but there is an expectation that function will improve. This is useful when there is a reason why performance is low. For Sheena, who remained in a confused state of PTA, yet had islands of preservation, I had every reason to expect improvement once PTA resolved. It is also my nature to be optimistic and certain that every individual can be the one to recover; this was how I approached Sheena.

In TV dramas a patient lies in a hospital bed in a coma, slowly opens her eyes, blinks in the harsh light and then says "Where am I?" and suddenly all normal cognitive skills return – speech, memory, verbal comprehension. That's not how it works. The brain injury patient wakes up to a near-impenetrable fog, and it is a function of that fog that the patient doesn't even know that it's there. But occasionally, even early on, a sudden shaft of daylight will shine through and then be closed off again.

So did Sheena know who I was? Yes and no. She couldn't have passed a test on it; but when she wasn't thinking about it she treated me as someone close and part of her life. And she knew ABOUT me, even if she couldn't quite pin me down.

Here's an example of this partial knowledge: in one of the first sessions we had with Gail Robinson, Sheena was being taken right back to the beginning of her life – her earliest memories from childhood. These were all fairly strong: where she'd lived, which primary school she had gone to, who her parents were, her brother and sister. Her teenage memories were intact too. The oldest memories were the most securely entrenched in her mind. "Did you do A levels? What subjects did you take?" Gail asked. "I did Scottish Highers," Sheena said, and remembered most of the subjects she'd taken. "Did you do well? Did you get good grades?" Gail asked. "Yes, they were quite good," Sheena said, and then shot a look across the room at me and said "Not as good as Allan, of course, but good enough."

It had been a running joke between us – that I'd got marginally better grades than her in our long forgotten school leaving exams. So here was the confusing thing: she seemed not to know who I was but she knew something as detailed and inconsequential as that. It made me think that the memories were not lost, just temporarily inaccessible, and that our challenge was to find them again.

Table 4.1 Sheena's short bedside neuropsychological assessment, March 1999

COGNITIVE DOMAINS Tests	12 March 1999 (14 days post-TBI)
PREMORBID INTELLECTUAL FUNCTIONING	
NART Equivalent IQ[1]	120 (Superior: 90th percentile)
INTELLECTUAL FUNCTIONS	
WAIS-R[2] Verbal IQ	75 (Borderline: <10th percentile)
Advanced Progressive Matrices[3]	7/12 (Average: 50–75th percentile)
MEMORY	
Orientation to person, place and time	PTA (disoriented)
Recognition memory test: words (short version)[4]	21/25 (Poor)
LANGUAGE FUNCTIONS	
Graded Naming Test: objects[5]	3/30 (Impaired range: <5th percentile)
Reading (NART)[1]	41/50 (Superior range: >90th percentile)
VISUAL PERCEPTION/ SPATIAL	
Incomplete letters test (VOSP[6])	Intact (19/20)
FRONTAL EXECUTIVE	
Similarities (WAIS-R[2])	Borderline impaired (concrete responses)
Colour Form Sorting: Weigl Test[7]	Pass (2/2)
Cognitive Estimates Test of Judgement[8]	Poor inappropriate responses
SPEED OF PROCESSING	
Number cancellation task[9]	Slow with many errors
QUALITATIVE OBSERVATIONS	Tangential, lose track of current task
RECOMMENDATIONS	
Use a diary to aid orientation and to track activities and visitors	

Notes: 1 Nelson and Willison (1991); 2 Wechsler (1981); 3 Raven (1990); 4 Warrington (1996); 5 Warrington (1997); 6 Warrington and James (1991); 7 Weigl (1941); 8 Shallice and Evans (1978); 9 Willison and Warrington (1992).

Friends, meaning well, suggested that I should take photographs in to try to fill in the missing years. I decided against this. I decided that I wouldn't tell her anything about our past. There was no point anyway since she wasn't laying down new memories and would forget again not long after being told. Instead I would encourage her to try to

*retrieve memories herself, and I would keep tabs on how successfully
she was doing this and on whether there was discernible improvement
as time went on.*

*I started bringing newspapers in. Sheena had always been surrounded
by the papers. I wanted her to start taking an interest again.*

*One day, my employers rang. I had been off work for weeks. They
suggested that it would be good for me to go back to work a day or two a
week. They asked whether I would like to present the Radio 4 programme*
The World Tonight *the following day. I'd done it before, filling in for the
regular presenters when they were on holiday. I said yes.*

*"I'm going to go back to work tomorrow," I told Sheena. "Just for a
day. But I don't have to start until the afternoon so I'll be in in the morning as usual."*

"OK," she said. Then, after a pause, "What sort of work is it you do?"

*This hurt, this really really hurt, and I felt the sting of it but tried not
to show it.*

"Well tomorrow I'm going to present The World Tonight *on Radio 4."*

"Will this come into it?" she said, picking up a copy of The Times. *The
front-page story was that the entire European Commission had resigned,
temporarily, while allegations of corruption were being investigated.
The former Labour leader, Neil Kinnock, was the UK's Commissioner at
the time and he was among those who had stepped down.*

"It might," I said, "it's quite a big story."

*"It seems implausible to me," she said. "I can't believe Neil Kinnock
has done anything corrupt."*

*I took this in. She had made a nuanced and reasoned judgement about
something in the news – without knowing that she was even in hospital!
And then, immediately, she said this:*

*"My sister's going to work for Radio 4 tomorrow, something to do
with the European Commission."*

*Although I had decided not to challenge or contradict anything she
said – I could see no merit in being confrontational – on this occasion,
very carefully, I corrected her. "No," I said, "That's me. I'm going to
work for Radio 4 tomorrow."*

*She looked genuinely affronted and apologetic. "Oh I'm so sorry,"
she said, almost formally, "I was muddling you up with my sister." By
now my heart was bursting. These were moments of great tenderness as
well as fear. And it's that that I remember more than anything.*

And then she said: "Will the people at Radio 4 know you're a doctor?"

*So it seemed to me that her head was a great churning kaleidoscope
of broken bits of knowledge turning over and tumbling around chaotically,*

unconnected shards of valid information and accurate recognition attaching themselves momentarily to the wrong thing and then detaching themselves again to continue the churn.

Gail told us, not long after Sheena's arrival at Queen Square, that she would do something called the Boston Naming Test. I sat and watched as Sheena was shown, one after another, a series of simple line drawings of everyday items that are easily recognisable – boy, cup, spoon, dog. Gail had 60 of these drawings. She stopped after 30. Sheena had scored three out of 30. And the effort of it had drained her of every ounce of energy. She was so tired she barely made it back to her bed.

Another new word entered my growing neurological lexicon: aphasia. Sheena appeared to know what these objects were, what they were for, but just couldn't recall their names. Would this lift? I asked. Would these words come back or would she have to relearn them all over again, as though learning the vocabulary of a foreign language? No-one knew.

Gail couldn't predict what would happen either:

> These tests represent a severe degree of intellectual under-functioning, with verbal skills most affected ... However, she is currently in a state of post- traumatic amnesia. At the present time, it would be beneficial for her to start using a diary to facilitate her daily memory in which appointments and visitors are noted and the current date is highlighted ...

And I tried. I have scratchy diary entries from only a few weeks after the injury – hard to read, hard to understand – but I was clearly anxious to please.

"Mum and Dianne (I have misspelt my sister-in-law's name) come to see me; exhausted by shower and seven bouquets of flowers. Earlier, fall asleep like Julia Somerville." I am perhaps already worrying about what people will think of me. TV journalist Julia Somerville had suffered a brain tumour, but eventually went back to work on television, and completely overcame any prejudice that insists brain-illness invariably leaves one unfit for life and work.

I persevered with the diary.

Saturday 13: "Pulled out drip, after lasting for two days. Allan Little visited – before pullout! Rod and Diane visit."

I disliked the nasogastric tube, and apparently kept pulling it out. I did not seem to know what my relationship with Allan was, since I referred to him formally.

Now Queen Square was the centre of my universe. I was still not allowed to enjoy the flowers that many people sent – not that I would have been aware of them; nor of the many get-well cards and letters that the hospital received. Visitors were not encouraged for many days, although when they finally were permitted by the family to spend a minute or two at my bedside, I am told that I received them graciously, and attempted conversations with everyone. I can only assume that being brought up to be polite was deeply ingrained.

Allan was very protective: he forbade my dear sister Alison (the family chronicler) from photographing me. Ironically, the first outsider and friend that he allowed into the ward was a photographer: Eve Arnold.

Eve Arnold was a household name in photography. She and Sheena were great friends and Eve had telephoned several times to check on Sheena's condition. I decided to ask Eve to come and visit. I knew she would play it straight. She wouldn't treat Sheena like an invalid. I asked her to come in the late morning and suggested that after the visit she and I go out to a local restaurant and have lunch.

Eve's latest book was called All in a Day's Work *and she had brought a copy to give to Sheena. It was a thoughtful gesture. Eve had seemed to understand that if Sheena lacked the sustained concentration to read, she might at least enjoy leafing through a collection of award winning photographs. Sheena tried to articulate something about the title, attempting to make the point that the photographs gathered there represented not a day's work but that of a long lifetime. I was touched to see Eve listening with great care, and understanding before I did what she was trying to say. "Yes you're right," she said to Sheena, and, later, to me: "She made a joke, a play on words. She'll be just fine."*

I walked Eve to the lifts. She was 88 years old, tiny, upright, ferociously intelligent and one of the most highly accomplished photographers in history. She looked at me expectantly: lunch? In almost any other circumstance it would have been a huge privilege for me to have an hour of Eve's company. But I couldn't do it. I shook my head and said "I don't think I can leave her." I think now that this was a mistake, that it would have been better, for Sheena as well as for me, for me to have carved out some more time away from the intensity of the hospital bedside, and to hold our friends closer and make them part of the process we were going through. But at the time I hadn't the heart for it. I watched Eve get in the lift and press the button for the ground floor and disappear. I wish now that I had gone with her.

Every day, my swallow was tested by Trish Gilpin. Every day, my family and Allan hoped that she would agree I could now eat. Day after day, she shook her head. "Not today." So I got thinner and thinner. My sister remembers me weighing around eight stone (about 50kg). Alas – the fashion-victim in me could not take compensatory pleasure from this state: I have no recollection of being underweight but fashionably slim! And there is nothing fashionable, anyway, about spending 24 hours a day, seven days a week, in a hospital bed. Every day, at mealtimes, the food-trolley came round the ward, and I have been told that I watched it being wheeled past my bed with greedy eyes.

I had not sprung back to what and where I was before I was hit. My recovery was uncertain, to say the least. My family and partner were not apprised of any likely prognosis.

A physiological overview reported that I was:

> Confused and disorientated. Wasn't sure where she was or why she was here. Confused about reasons for nasal tube. Normal muscle-tone. Able to stand independently and walk forwards and backwards with minimal assistance. Gait pattern is mildly ataxic.

In other words, although I could now stand and walk a little, I was unable to walk in a straight line. So I could totter back and forth, but could not swallow or make any sense, either in understanding what was happening or expressing it.

My weight was now down to 60kg. Over four weeks had passed since food had passed my lips. I was dependent on Trish Gilpin's assessment of my swallow. The serious reason behind her careful daily observation was that the body, in recovery, can confuse the oesophagus with the windpipe. One allows air into the body through breathing, the second food through eating and drinking. Mistaking the two involuntarily can be very dangerous. No-one wants to inhale porridge, or ice-cream, or fruit.

Exactly two weeks later, the Boston Naming Test was repeated. This time Sheena had the energy for all 60. She scored well early on. But the drawings got a little more difficult (though not much). Gail showed her a picture of a helicopter. Sheena's brow furrowed, as she struggled to find the word. "Aeroplane. . . ?" she said tentatively and I could tell she knew that wasn't quite right. But it was consistent with Gail's earlier reading: that she knew what things did even if she didn't know what they were called. Some people have the opposite problem – knowing what things are called but having no grasp of what they are for or what they do.

Then Sheena was shown a picture of the Great Pyramid at Giza. She struggled again. "It's something to do with the shape," Gail said. "Triangle. . . ?" said Sheena and I could see again that she knew this wasn't right.

"Where do you find this thing?" Gail asked.

"In the desert," said Sheena.

"I was thinking about a particular country," said Gail.

"Well, Egypt of course!" said Sheena and rolled her eyes as if to say "Does this woman think I'm an idiot?" It was a golden moment. My heart leapt. It was vintage Sheena. She's in there, I thought, she's not lost, she'll be back. Thus do you invest small moments with great meaning. It helps to keep you going.

Months later we met a former England Rugby International who was also recovering from a brain injury and had suffered aphasia. He described repainting his son's bedroom. He'd forgotten the word "decorating". "I've been upstairs," he told someone who telephoned, "making the rooms better."

We would spend five weeks in Queen Square and gradually I would let a few people in to see her for a few minutes at a time. I watched Sheena make conversation with them, actively trying to disguise her ongoing condition. Each visit – though it lasted only a few minutes – left her exhausted and she would lapse again, after the visitor had left, into dreamtalk and then sleep.

The therapy continued. "We want to test her executive function," an occupational therapist said. This would involve taking Sheena to a kitchen a little way down the corridor from the ward to see whether she knew how to use basic kitchen implements.

Again I sat by the empty bed and waited. When Sheena came back she was shattered and, once she'd been helped into bed, collapsed.

They took me way, way along a long corridor. I had to climb THREE FLIGHTS of stairs and then back down TWO MORE flights. We got into a kitchen and they asked for a cup of tea and a ham sandwich. So I made them a cup of tea and a ham sandwich – but it was a complete waste of time, because when I'd done it, no-one wanted it!

She was speaking whole sentences now that made sense. But she still had no clear insight into the fact that she was in hospital and being treated for the effect of a brain injury. There was still no past, and no future, within which to place this long, never-ending present. And still no cognitive ability to question why she was making tea and sandwiches for complete strangers.

When she fell asleep I walked along the corridor to the kitchen. The three flights of stairs she'd had to walk up were in fact three steps, barely noticeable to someone in normal health. But they'd felt to Sheena like three storeys to climb.

My mother was day and daily by my bedside, as was Allan, who was now staying in a friend's flat. I remember nothing about their presence. My sister-in-law Diane still spent the weekends staying with my mother. Diane said:

"Before going back to work on Monday. I remember lying on Sheena's bed with her, and just chatting and sometimes laughing – just trying to help her communicate. Sheena would always be pulling out her feeding tube and the nurses continually re-inserted it.

"On one occasion Sheena introduced me to the nurse, saying, 'This is my wife.'

"On seeing Allan she asked me, 'Who is that?' 'It's Allan, your boyfriend,' I said. 'Do I know him?' 'Well, I think so.'

"She came back from a word test looking forlorn, saying she 'only got a couple right'. It was going to be a long road back."

It was now over four weeks since the injury. I do not use the word "accident"; driving on the wrong side of the road is not done accidentally. I am told that I was able to walk around the ward with supervision "due to unsteadiness". I could get from my bed to the chair next to it with help. I didn't understand the need for shower-curtains, and I had to sit down to put on trousers, pants, shoes.

My speech and language functions were reassessed, and I was doing better. My auditory comprehension of grammar was 100%, and I was getting better at naming everyday objects, although the assessor noted that I was tired and could not do the whole test. I still could not swallow fluids without coughing.

There was conversation about sending me to another institution to improve my language skills. I was unaware of this. I was also unaware of how my facial injuries were healing. I have no recollection of using a mirror.

Language and aphasia

Language is one of the most obvious indicators of cognitive functioning. It is the bridge between people, the way we communicate. When the different aspects of language work together in harmony, it is our way to tell stories and communicate our desires, needs and knowledge. This was noticed by Allan immediately as the content of Sheena's speech was not characteristic: it reflected disturbance to several cognitive functions.

How do we assess the different aspects of language? First, does speech sound like speech? Are the sounds recognisable and well-articulated? Is it the same for single words and sentences? Are sentences complete with grammar? Are sentences produced with intonation or a melody of speech, or does speech sound flat, like a monotone voice? These are questions I ask that focus on pure *speech production* and *fluency*. Sheena's speech production and fluency were good from early on, even when still in PTA. By contrast, when I asked if the sentences made sense, it was clear that coherence of spontaneous speech were poor (e.g., Barker *et al.*, 2017). This is related to the aspect of language associated with the frontal lobe; namely, *spontaneous speech*. This involves the ability to generate an idea, which is voluntary and novel to any given context, and express it in spoken language (Luria, 1973). When this is disturbed it results in *frontal dynamic aphasia*, in which patients have language skills but they do not speak or use it to communicate (for detailed case studies see Luria, 1970; Robinson *et al.*, 1998; 2005; 2015). Although Sheena's spontaneous speech was not normal, it was not consistent with this pattern of frontal dynamic aphasia.

Sheena's difficulties at this acute stage appeared when attempting to retrieve a specific word. It was apparent in everyday conversations and is assessed formally with picture naming tests. Word finding difficulties are also known as *nominal aphasia* (Mayer and Murray, 2003). If a specific word is not retrieved, it may be that a description is given instead that indicates the object is known (circumlocution e.g., the flying object that carries people to a destination – for helicopter), or sometimes a different name is retrieved that is semantically related (e.g., aeroplane for helicopter). Occasionally the cause may be that a person simply does not know the item or they perceive it visually as a different item (e.g., binoculars for handcuffs). Knowledge of items, comprehending grammar and understanding abstract concepts are aspects of language that are integral not only for naming objects, but for conversation and communication.

To their great credit and my huge relief none of the medical staff who treated her ever talked to her as though she were an invalid. If anyone did she picked up on it instantly. A food nutritionist came to see her. She had not eaten for weeks and was getting painfully thin and physically frail.

"I understand you were complaining the other day of being hungry,"
the woman said, gently and sympathetically.
"Oh I wasn't complaining," Sheena said. "I was merely observing."
In the privacy of my own head this made me smile. The comment was vin-
tage Sheena. It seemed to me the shards of her personality – the pre-injury
Sheena would not have wanted anyone to think she was "complaining" –
were in there and bit by bit were piecing themselves back together into the
single consummate whole. It was like being in the presence of a miracle.

After two weeks in the National, I was "much more awake", my short-
term memory was "fair", and, despite extensive bruising, I reported
no limb or face pain any more. The catheter was removed, and I could
transfer to a commode with help. My pneumothorax problem had been
resolved at UCH, and the chest-drain had been removed, leaving a little scar. I still had a considerable blind spot in my right field vision, so
did not see very well, and wore an eye-patch over my right eye. I was
deemed to be cooperative and drowsy, but easily roused.

Finally, there came a significant breakthrough: I could finally swallow –
imperfectly, but well enough to be fed three half-pots of yoghurt a day. Still
no fluids, but Allan was permitted to spoon-feed me. My nasogastric tube
remained in. Eating was tiring, and the hospital wanted to be sure I was getting the basic nutritional minimum.

Sheena had lost a lot of weight. After four weeks Trish Gilpin repeated
her "swallow test". It was a Thursday afternoon and we stood around
the bed waiting in anticipation. If she didn't pass this test – Trish didn't
work on Fridays – there wouldn't be another one till Monday. Trish
shook her head. No. Sheena's swallow still wasn't strong enough. That
sign, Nil By Mouth, would stay up and Sheena would have another four
days without eating, being fed through a nasal tube that she kept, without
realising she was doing it, pulling out.
The following Monday she was deemed fit enough to eat. The afternoon
trolley came round the ward. A plastic plate was set in front of Sheena.
The food was beige. Beige potatoes. Beige bits of chicken. "If she hasn't
eaten in a while, make sure she doesn't wolf it," the hospital orderly said.
I had always noted, with admiration, that the medics almost never
addressed Sheena as though she were an invalid, but spoke directly to
her as an adult with respect. They never spoke ABOUT her while she
was there to listen.
This was an exception. "If she hasn't eaten in a while, make sure she
doesn't wolf it." Sheena picked up on this immediately and I saw the old

defiance in the way she clocked the orderly as she moved on to the next bed. Sheena waited till she was out of earshot then looked down at the most unappetising plate of food I'd ever seen. "She's bloody hopeful if she thinks I'm going to wolf this," she said. I laughed out loud for the first time. Another tick: first barbed rejoinder; first successfully articulated witticism. Progress!

My father wrote a poem to commemorate these miniature landmarks:

She lies quietly – youthful face.

Wonderfully smiling when Allan speaks and strokes her head.

Her face leans out eagerly for the spoonful of yoghurt.

She walks with aid down the ward.

Face grey and drawn with weariness when she comes back.

Scratches at the tube that feeds nourishment through the nose.

Worries over finance, and the form her career will take – and when.

Fears she is boring.

No longer says – Going home now.

I have no recollection of keeping a diary, but when I look at my scrawled notes now, I seem to be becoming more coherent: "After lunch, Belinda and Simon Gallimore came – and Sue Inglish. Tony Palmer dropped by. All good value. Physio gave instruction on stiff finger. Lost mouth-pipe and nasal tube – hurray!"

"Wednesday 24: Woke up 2.30, 4.30, 6.30 – finally allowed to shower at 7.20, when day-staff replace night-staff. Breakfast: real food – Weetabix and cold tea. Busy morning: physiologist, psychologist, occupational therapist, all taking notes. Psychologist did death and disaster quiz – hopeless! I knew nothing. She couldn't pronounce questions."

What Sheena called the "death and disaster" quiz was enlightening in its own way. She was shown a series of pictures and newspaper headlines from the period of her own lifetime and asked whether she could identify them: the assassination of JFK; the Falklands War; Vietnam; the election of Margaret Thatcher; the fall of the Berlin Wall. I could see, though I think the therapist could not, that she vaguely recognised these events but did not say so because she thought she was being quizzed on them at a much higher level and was reluctant to say any-thing unless she could talk about them at length and in depth – which was still way beyond her powers of recall and linguistic fluency. "Who's the Prime Minister?" the therapist asked. Tony Blair had been elected fewer than two years earlier. Sheena had known the Blairs personally for years; they'd sent flowers from 10 Downing Street to the Intensive Care Unit the day after her injury had become public knowledge. She couldn't recall his name so – again I could see it but the therapist could not – decided to disguise this shortcoming by making light if it. "Oh, some young lad," she said dismissively.

By now I was beginning to see that there were things about her condition that I was picking up that the tests were not. More of the pre-injury Sheena was functioning – I could see the traits – than the tests were reg-istering. I began to understand that I could and would play a part in the recovery process, not because I had any expertise in the field (manifestly I had none) but because I had something that the medics did not. I knew her and could see when she was dissembling or disguising or diverting, and knew that her ability to do all of these things was in itself improving all the time. I don't think the tests that were being run, important though they were, picked much of that up.

It's only now that I write this, nearly 20 years on, that I wonder why I was left to my own devices. I remember no attempt, until much later, to draw me into the recovery effort, no real attempt to guide me or advise me or even to ask me for my own observations. The families of brain injury survivors play a huge role in the recovery. It seems odd to me now that for the most part I devised my own strategies almost completely unaided.

So I seemed to be becoming more self-aware. This is illusory, in that I was still not laying down new memories. If I had not spidered the follow-ing notes, I would not know that these things, mundane as they are, ever happened, nor that various friends had been so solicitous.

"Monday 29: Carol Leppard, Gramophone, phoned. Woke early, show-ered at 7.15. Visited library – then slept again – veggy supper. Ma left."

I remember the significance of that phone call and it amazes me. Not much over a month after my injury, I am telling the organiser of the annual Gramophone Awards that I will be capable of presenting a high-profile evening event in the autumn at the Royal Festival Hall in London before 2,000 people – and she is believing me.

Although technically "conscious" for the previous five weeks, I have almost no memory of that time, and no understanding of what had happened.

Today, I am fascinated and intrigued by one of neurology's ongoing teasers: what IS consciousness – as opposed to self-awareness coupled with personal memory and identity?

Dr. Greenwood's latest assessment was guarded: "She still has significant problems processing information . . . and will need some sort of 24-hour supervision for the next several weeks." I continued to complain of blurred vision. I was referred to the eye-clinic. The assessment was inconclusive. "Watch closely" was the main advice.

The physiologist noted that my broken left middle finger was swollen and hot. There was some concern that it had not healed correctly, and another X-ray was requested. How this digit was broken and no other limb may seem mysterious, but later I guessed that the large ring I wore on that finger had somehow got caught and the finger had eventually broken under pressure. Much later, I was given what was found of the ring – a twisted silver setting with the agate stone missing.

So I was conscious, I could converse, I was polite and co-operative – but I had no idea I existed. I was apparently performing an increasingly plausible impersonation of someone called Sheena McDonald – but that person, as she knew herself and the world around her, was not there. I am told that I did not question why I was shuffling, feeling exhausted, was being encouraged to wear an eye-patch and had a poor memory. I passively and submissively tottered around my tiny new world. I began to realise, confusedly, that I was not well, but that I would be all right – perhaps a product of Allan reiterating this assurance to me time and again.

I was not sure exactly who Allan was, but I was sure I knew him well, and that I did not expect to see him there. I must have expected him, whoever he was, to be abroad. As long as I had known him, he had lived abroad. And here he was, two days running. Three days running. Of course, he was a doctor – I did know that.

But he said he wasn't. I wondered why he had not taken up medicine, since he had studied it. (In fact, he had not – he studied history, and became a journalist.)

Gradually, I learned a version of the events that have led up to my new life.

My retrograde amnesia remained, as though events and individuals and names had simply been erased from the slate. To this day, I have to look up an old appointments diary to find out what I was doing, and what I was supposed to be doing before a police-van got in the way. It told me that every coming day was filled to bursting-point with engagements and commitments and contracts.

My level of motor independence was beginning to improve. I washed, dressed and went to the loo unaided. I was told that I could walk out of doors, under supervision.

"This hospital," Sheena said one day, about five weeks after the injury. "Is it new or old?" I was excited by this question for two reasons. First, it was just about the first time she'd initiated a conversation herself, so it revealed to me that there was a curiosity about her surroundings that had not been there before and a new willingness to ask questions about the world around her. And second, it was the first time (incredible though this sounds) that she had acknowledged, unprompted, that she was in hospital. I tried to stay casual.

"Well," I said, "I think it's an old hospital but this wing is quite new because there's a plaque downstairs that says it was opened by Princess Diana." Princess Diana had died two years earlier.

"Ah yes, I met her once," Sheena said.

"What do you know about Princess Diana?" I said.

"She's been unlucky I think," said Sheena.

"What with?"

"Um. . . her children. . . ?" This was a guess. Clearly Princess Diana had been far from unlucky with her children.

"What else?" I asked.

"I think she's withdrawn from public life hasn't she?" Sheena said.

Again, very casually I broke my own rule. "Actually Princess Diana has died," I said.

Sheena looked shocked. "What? When? How?" This was good to hear. Clearly the memory was still shot away but this engagement with the world, this concern, this clearly emotional reaction, this curiosity were all new.

"A couple of years ago. She was in a car crash in Paris," I said.

Sheena furrowed her brow and said "Oh no! That's terrible. How sad."

She looked perplexed for a minute as though trying to make sense of something and then turned to me and said "You know, I don't think that's widely known."

I had to stifle a laugh. She must have been the only person in the world to have forgotten the death of Princess Diana. "It was in some of the newspapers at the time," I said.

But to me it was all progress, all to be celebrated. The retrograde amnesia was still there. The inability to lay down new memories was still there. But there was a growing engagement with the world and a growing ability to articulate thoughts and ideas and – crucially – a new ability to initiate. Sheena would quickly forget having that conversation; but, in time, the memory of Princess Diana's death would return along with most of the "missing years".

Frontal "executive" functions: initiation and inhibition

Initiation of behaviour is crucial to *do* anything, without a prompt or responding to something outside of ourselves; that is, *internally generated* vs. *externally driven* responses. As noted before, this relates to the anterior (or frontal)/ posterior divide in the brain. Initiation is an indicator that Sheena's executive functions were beginning to engage. As this occurs and initiation begins, it is also the case that *impulsiveness* can increase at the same time. This means that an impulse to do something arises, with initiation, but it is not always the case that *inhibition* of inappropriate responses operates to monitor response quality or appropriateness. When executive functions are fully working, there is a balance between initiation and inhibition. At this point behaviours are initiated and executed, like attempting to walk when balance is poor, which may result in risky or unsafe behaviours.

My latest prognosis was realistic: "Given the site of her head-injury, Sheena may have some high level executive problems in initiating, planning and organising. . . ." On the brighter side, "Sheena has good insight into her problems and therefore has good potential to learn strategies to overcome them."

I had one last week to spend at the National.

I am often asked about "coming to". It happened in a very piecemeal way, not all of a sudden. It most certainly was not a case of "gone today, here tomorrow". My early memories are fragmentary and occasional, and looking back seems akin to being an archaeologist, and trying to deduce what the whole pot would have looked like from the shard of broken china dug up. My entire life seemed like a pell-mell assortment of bits of broken china – yet I did not seem to care all that much about my new condition.

My experience of post-traumatic amnesia was estimated as lasting for five weeks – an untypically long duration – indicating head-injury in the "extremely severe" category.

I persisted with my efforts to tease out her memory. "I want her to remember where we were at Christmas and New Year, two months before the injury," I'd say to friends. "Then why don't you show her some photographs?" they'd reply.

That wasn't how I wanted the memories to come back. So I said to her, "Try to remember where we were at New Year." She said she would think about it and try to remember by the end of the week. This too was progress, because implicitly she was acknowledging now that she had memory problems and she was agreeing to participate in her own recovery. She also seemed to know and trust me now.

The end of that week was Easter weekend. I suggested we go for a walk along the corridor past the little hospital chapel. There was a service taking place. The sound of a choir filled the corridor as we approached. It triggered something in her mind. "I've remembered where we were at New Year," she said. "We went to that funny little Anglican Church in Moscow for a midnight service. I thought the vicar was a bit drunk!"

I almost punched the air. I was delirious with joy. That was how it would be from now on, I thought. Sheena would participate in her now recovery and memory would come flooding back organically as her brain settled down.

I had no idea what a long and difficult road lay ahead.

My optimism got ahead of reality. One day an occupational therapist said she wanted to take Sheena out onto the street into the bustle of the city to see how she coped. I was tremendously excited by this. The problem was she had no shoes. The shoes she had been wearing on the night of the injury had been cut off and thrown away. "We'll do it another day, when you've brought some shoes in," the therapist said. In my impatience I said I'd run down to Oxford Street and buy some shoes: I wanted this done today. She said she would be going off duty soon, so I sprinted down Southampton Row and along New Oxford Street, my heart thumping against my rib cage, and ran into the first shoe shop I came upon. I didn't want to let this chance slip away, or for it to be delayed even by a day.

I bought a pair of tennis shoes in Sheena's size and sprinted back. Sheena was dressed and ready but still didn't really know exactly what for. She was still not able to grasp what a big deal walking out into the street was for her.

The therapist told her to go into a shop and buy a newspaper and a packet of crisps. Straightforward though this sounds, many brain injury survivors struggle with simple tasks like this. Sheena managed it without difficulty.

But again, when she came back to the ward, the effort had worn her out.
She slept for the rest of the day.
I asked a few days later whether I could take her out for lunch.
There was a little Italian restaurant about 200 yards from the front
door of the hospital. I was excited about the prospect of sitting down
at a restaurant table with Sheena again. It took an age to get there.
Sheena was unsteady on her feet and still painfully slow. When we got
to the restaurant she looked at the menu and we ordered a couple of
bowls of pasta. It was hopelessly, woefully unrealistic. By the time the
food arrived she was beyond exhausted, far too tired even to pick up
a fork, never mind eat. I had to send both dishes back to a dismayed
chef, pay, and begin a long and painful 200-yard stagger back to the
hospital. It was an important lesson. You have to prepare yourself not
to get carried away by a seeming return to something approaching
normality and to remember that this process is going to take a very
long time indeed.

After five weeks at Queen Square, Dr. Greenwood said that I was "ready for neurological rehabilitation". I was now scoring 51 out of 60 in the classic naming test. I was designated as "significantly improving", although I was still having difficulty finding words, still having some difficulty swallowing, and still in need of "some supervision to avoid mild impulsiveness". Physically, my right cheek remained swollen, but the doctors seemed satisfied with its progress.

My finger was deemed to be progressing, but needed physiotherapy – it might take "some months to acquire suppleness".

Dr. Greenwood suggested the possibility of my going to the Astley Ainslie Hospital in Edinburgh, with a view, eventually, to moving back into my flat in the city. It had finally been established that my GP was in Edinburgh, and I therefore qualified to undergo "intensive cognitive rehabilitation" at the Astley Ainslie. If more work were needed, I might be transferred to the Oliver Zangwill Unit for cognitive rehabilitation in Ely.

References

Badre, D. (2008). "Cognitive control, hierarchy, and the rostro-caudal organization of the frontal lobes". *Trends in Cognitive Science*, 12(5), 193–200.

Baird, A., Papadopoulou, K., Greenwood, R. and Cipolotti, L. (2005). "Memory function after resolution of post-traumatic amnesia". *Brain Injury*, 19, 811–817.

Barker M.S., Young, B. and Robinson, G.A. (2017). "Cohesive and coherent connected speech deficits in mild stroke". *Brain and Language*, 168, 23–36.

Cipolotti, L. and Warrington, E.K. (1995). "Neuropsychological assessment". *Journal of Neurology, Neurosurgery and Psychiatry*, 58(6), 655–664.

Diamond A. (2013). "Executive Functions". *Annual Review of Psychology*, 64, 135–168.

Guy, S., Clarke, L., Bryant, H., Robinson, G., Segaran, E., Losseff, N. and Stewart, T. (2004). "An interdisciplinary team approach to acute stroke rehabilitation". *Neurological Rehabilitation of Stroke*, 23–48.

Lezak, M.D., Howieson, D.B., Loring, D.W. and Fischer, J.S. (2004). *Neuropsychological Assessment*. New York, NY: Oxford University Press.

Luria, A. R. (1970). *Traumatic Aphasia*. The Hague: Mouton.

Luria, A.R. (1973). *The Working Brain* (trans: Haigh, B.). London: Penguin Books.

Mayer, J. and Murray, L. (2003). "Functional measures of naming in aphasia: word retrieval in confrontation naming versus connected speech". *Aphasiology*, 17(5), 481–497.

Nelson, H. and Willison, J. (1991). *The National Adult Reading Test*, 2nd edition. Windsor: The NFER-Nelson Publishing Co. Ltd.

Norman, D.A. and Shallice, T. (1986). "Attention to action". Chapter 1 in R.J. Davidson, G.E. Schwartz and D. Shapiro (eds), *Consciousness and Self-regulation* (pp. 1–18). Boston, MA: Springer.

Raven J. (1990). *Advanced Progressive Matrices Sets I and II*. Oxford: Oxford Psychologists Press Ltd.

Robinson, G., Blair, J. and Cipolotti, L. (1998). "Dynamic aphasia: an inability to select between competing verbal responses?" *Brain*, 121, 77–89.

Robinson, G., Shallice, T. and Cipolotti, L. (2005). "A failure of high level verbal response selection in progressive dynamic aphasia". *Cognitive Neuropsychology*, 22(6), 661–694.

Robinson, G.A., Spooner, D. and Harrison, W.J. (2015). "Frontal dynamic aphasia in progressive supranuclear palsy: distinguishing between generation and fluent sequencing of novel thoughts". *Neuropsychologia*, 77, 62–75.

Shallice, T. and Burgess, P.W. (1991). "Deficits in strategy application following frontal lobe damage in man". *Brain*, 114(2), 727–741.

Shallice, T. and Evans, M.E. (1978). "The involvement of the frontal lobes in cognitive estimation". *Cortex*, 14(2), 294–303.

Stuss, D.T. (2011). "Functions of the frontal lobes: relation to executive functions". *Journal of the International Neuropsychological Society*, 17, 759–765.

Warrington, E. (1996). *The Camden Memory Tests: Topographical Recognition Memory Test*. East Sussex: Psychology Press.

Warrington E. (1997). "The Graded Naming Test: a restandardisation". *Neuropsychological Rehabilitation*, 7, 143–146.

Warrington, E. and James, M. (1991). *Visual Object and Space Perception Battery*. London: Thames Valley Test Company.

Wechsler, D. (1981). *Wechsler Adult Intelligence Scale-Revised*. San Antonio, TX: The Psychological Corporation.

Weigl, E. (1941). "On the psychology of so-called processes of abstraction". *Journal of Normal and Social Psychology*, 36, 3–33.

Willison, J.R. and Warrington, E.K. (1992). "Cognitive retardation in a patient with preservation of psychomotor speed". *Behavioural Neurology*, 5(2), 113–116.

Zigmond, A.S. and Snaith, R.P. (1983). "The hospital anxiety and depression scale". *Acta Psychiatrica Scandinavica*, 67(6), 361–370.

Chapter 5

Who am I now?

I was discharged from the National Hospital in Queen Square in London on 6 April 1999, and travelled by rail to Edinburgh with Allan.

I wanted to get Sheena back to Edinburgh, our home city. We were now thinking about how to make the transition from hospital to living at home. Sheena wasn't ready for that yet but I knew that when the time came, this would be much easier in Edinburgh.

We took a taxi from Queen Square to Kings Cross and got on the train. The four-and-a-half hour journey was exhausting for Sheena. I was worried about how she was going to get off the train. The hospital, to my surprise and relief, had anticipated this and had arranged for a car to be driven onto the station platform at precisely the place where the train coach we were travelling in would come to a halt. Sheena staggered the short distance from train to car looking fragile and drawn. A newspaper photographer snapped the moment – and there we were, the next morning, on the front pages of the red tops again.

The hospital car drove us directly to the Astley Ainsley Hospital on the south side of the city.

Post-acute neurorehabilitation: the journey home

The post-acute neurorehabilitation process is similar to that at the acute stage; however, a patient is able to engage and participate to a greater degree and can set goals along with family and the multidisciplinary team. Cognitive, behavioural, physical, social and emotional consequences of brain injury are intrinsically linked and considered (see Figure 5.1; adapted from Wilson and Gracey, 2009).

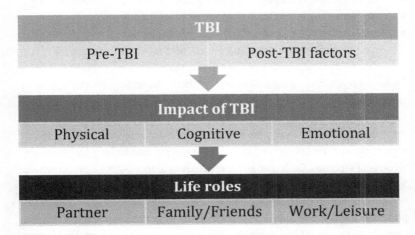

Figure 5.1 The impact of a TBI on an individual and life roles

Once a patient recovers to the point where they are able to engage in neuro-rehabilitation, like Sheena now at the Astley Ainslie, it is possible to complete a fuller neuropsychological assessment that includes cognition, behaviour and mood. Interventions can target cognitive and behavioural disturbances, as well as practical tasks that allow an individual to be independent in self-care (e.g., walking, washing, shopping). Increasingly at this stage, psychosocial or emotional concerns are instrumental in the neurorehabilitation process. An overall sum-mary of the organic damage, pre- and post-TBI factors, and cognitive strengths and weaknesses can provide a useful account of the immediate problems, which can then highlight where to start with interventions.

Approaches to neurorehabilitation

There are different approaches to neurorehabilitation, which influence multi-disciplinary teams and individual health professionals. Intervention strategies range widely, for example:

- environmental management strategies (as detailed in Chapter 4 for man-aging agitation and confusion in the acute stage of rehabilitation);
- restitution, substitution or compensation techniques, depending on the severity and degree of function lost;

- use of learning techniques (e.g., errorless learning, procedural learning);
- psychotherapy for managing emotional reactions;
- psychoeducation to understand what has happened;
- psychological interventions (e.g., cognitive behavioural therapy).

These interventions receive different emphasis depending on the approach taken. Cognitive rehabilitation has a focus on techniques to restore, substitute or compensate for cognitive impairments. Behavioural approaches tend to focus on explicit and implicit learning techniques; for example, errorless learning strengthens the correct response and minimises interference by eliminating incorrect responses. Both cognitive and behavioural approaches typically include a psychoeducational component in order to understand what a TBI is and how it impacts the brain and individual. Holistic neurorehabilitation approaches incorporate all of these techniques in addition to emphasising psychotherapeutic approaches that target self-awareness and adjustment to a new post-TBI identity.

I arrived with this discharge summary from the National:

> She was run over by a police van. Head injury, frontal contusions, zygoma, facial and middle finger. Was admitted to UCH. Cognitive decline/poor memory. Blurred vision in the right eye. Seen by the neuro-ophthalmologist, who reassured her and said it will improve. To see her in three months time. Condition continues to improve.

It went on to detail what medication I was on, and to warn against saying anything about my condition if the press should call.

All in all, my state was considered to be better than expected – which is to say, I was having no seizures, had no problem breathing, was mobilising independently, was no longer in pain, and was "self-caring with hygiene needs".

But I was still experiencing "word-finding difficulties" and "double vision". Under "General Assessment" they had written "Frustrated. Tired. Can be impulsive – needs some supervision. Retrograde memory loss. Short-term memory problems. Facial scars. Chest drain wound being dressed. Is able to tell you if she knows name of person calling or visiting."

The Astley Ainslie Hospital is in south Edinburgh, near to where I grew up. It is part of the Lothian Primary Care NHS Trust. It provides rehabilitation services for adults with acquired brain injury, amongst other conditions.

The hospital is spread over several buildings. It lies in a small park. One had to walk across lawns and under trees to reach the buildings where the therapy was given. At the time, it seemed to me I was having to walk long distances between locations. Years later I went back – and the buildings were in fact fairly close together. Of course. In 1999, every normal, mundane activity seemed to need great effort, whether it was walking, or climbing stairs, or swallowing, or reading. I was determined to do as well as I could at all the tests and assessments they gave me – a determination undermined by my actual abilities.

I was in the neurological ward on the second floor of the Charles Bell Pavilion. My consultant was Dr. Brian Pentland, a direct, no-nonsense Scot. The ward was filled with similar sufferers. At first untrained sight, many seemed much worse off than me – unable to speak or walk. Joy of joys – I was given a single side-room. I was still on the main neurological ward in the Charles Bell Pavilion, but had my own tiny bedroom, with en-suite shower.

There were many people far more badly injured than Sheena and again the nature of brain injury – the cruel randomness of it – came home to me. What determines most how a survivor will recover? Luck, I thought – whether your brain had been hit head on, and ricocheted inside your skull in a straight line, or whether the impact had been "rotational", twisting the brain inside your skull and sheering the brain stem from the tissue to which it was connected could make the difference between returning to a normal life and being permanently disabled. And that in turn was determined by something as random as the position your head happened to be in when the impact occurred.

I was to spend three weeks here. I was now allowed to receive flowers, unlike in London, and also visitors. My old boyfriend John (with whom I had confused Allan) regularly phoned from Australia. Allan was now back to occasional work in London, so phoned the ward every day he was away. He had never called daily before the injury. Now, not a day passed without conversation. Our lives had changed.

I was assessed at my new hospital. I was asked to say where I was, and what the day and date were. Then I was asked to repeat the names of objects given to me, to name illustrations of objects, to do simple mental arithmetic. The hospital informed my general practitioner of my condition thus far. My ongoing problems included cognitive impairment which affected my attention-span, memory, complex visuo-spatial reasoning, verbal reasoning and verbal fluency. I was still receiving medication – a daily dose of Omeprazole.

I underwent physiotherapy, occupational therapy and psychotherapy. The physiotherapy was for my finger, which was still strengthening. I was given a splint, in an attempt to straighten the swollen, bent digit, and encouraged to bend it as far as it would go, in order to be as near normal again. The occupational therapy was to acclimatise me back into a thinking world, and involved performing everyday activities, like cooking and cleaning. Initially, I was reported to have difficulty following written instructions. I finally graduated to interviewing, one of my erstwhile skills as a journalist. My therapist asked me to interview a couple of her colleagues about the challenges of being working parents.

"I don't really do personality interviews," I said.

She rolled her eyes.

"You are so demanding!"

The psychotherapy always started with 30 minutes on the exercycle. I enjoyed and appreciated this. Before the injury, I often felt that an invisible band ran between my legs and brain. If I ever ran short of ideas, or the *mot juste*, a simple stroll round the block would invariably pull an appropriate rabbit out of the hat. Now, I felt energised by cycling, and ready to be put through my paces. I was tested on short-term memory loss by being asked to repeat back random strings of numbers. I could remember six or seven with ease, but eight or nine was always a problem. I had to name objects, repeat stories, extemporise on unrelated themes: each test was designed to reveal exactly which part of my brain was still suffering.

I showed signs of improvement. I reportedly learned to "initiate more" and "offer more information" but my learning memory and visual memory were all "impaired". My consultant Dr. Pentland held off on deciding whether I should be sent to another institution for further intensive psychotherapy once I left the Astley Ainslie. I would need full-time supervision. Allan volunteered to take two or three months off work.

My insight was still "limited" but "increasing", which they feared "might cause problems with mood". They were right, although it would be more than a year before I was diagnosed as clinically depressed.

Word-finding difficulty (nominal dysphasia) was an irritating but somewhat amusing ongoing problem. One day, I was talking to Allan about – now what is that little furry pet animal called?

"Cashew?" I said tentatively. I was looking for the word "hamster".

I certainly could not go back to broadcasting – if anyone would hire me – until I felt more confident with language. But before the injury I had agreed to present an edition of *International Question Time* for the BBC World Service at the Commonwealth Heads of Government

Meeting in Durban in November, fewer than nine months after being felled. That was my goal.

Much later, when I was shown my medical notes for this stay in a third hospital, I discovered I had also been given speech therapy. Apparently I became better at reading out loud, but was "frustrated that [my] speed of reading is slow". This may have been due to my eye-damage.

Reading my notes later, I learned that I was also slow to comprehend instructions. My family was advised not to pressurise me. A hospital goal was to enable me fully to understand visual or auditory communication, then to be independent in personal and social affairs and to problem-solve independently – along with improving my memory and word-finding abilities, both still very approximate. All the staff reported that I needed extra time to problem-solve, and repetition of information.

After a couple of weeks in the Astley Ainslie, it was recommended that I attempt a weekend home-visit – that is, to spend two days and a night at my own first-floor flat in the centre of Edinburgh, with the proviso that Allan be in constant attendance. I could now use the bed, chair, toilet and shower competently. So I went home. I actually spent most of that weekend sleeping.

Our Edinburgh flat was a "double upper" – the first and second floors of what had been a four-storey townhouse that had at some time in the past been divided into two separate homes. The first thing you had to do from street level was climb a flight of stairs to the main living floor. To get to the bathroom you had to climb another set of stairs.

Even before Sheena came home I was terrified of the stairs. She was so unsteady on her feet that I was sure this was a major hazard. If left to her own devices it would just be a matter of time before she stumbled on the stairs and fell. I knew she couldn't be left alone even for a few minutes and that first weekend I began to understand how much of Sheena's need for constant care while her recovery continued would fall to me. Her swallow was still so poor that I had to make her promise not to try to eat anything unless I was in the room.

We had a near miss early on: during one meal, Sheena took a forkful of pasta and instead of swallowing it, it lodged deep in her windpipe, cutting off her breathing altogether. She looked at me in distress and indicated what had happened but without breathing couldn't utter a sound. I knew I had only a few moments to dislodge the inhaled food and I haphazardly turned her upside down and thumped her on the back between the shoulder blades until she expelled the food and her whole torso shook with the effort of gasping for breath. It was a terrifying moment.

Not exactly the Heimlich manoeuvre, it's true, but it worked, and it was a lesson in just how dependent Sheena would be for a long time to come on constant supervision.

The home-visit was deemed sufficiently successful to trigger a discharge-date. This was set for the end of my third week at the Astley Ainslie. I would thereafter be treated as an outpatient. My swallowing was better, although I still occasionally confused my oesophagus and windpipe, and had a coughing fit.

I was reported to be "calm and assured" but to wish "further improvement to occur at a faster pace". And I behaved "appropriately" with staff and family.

Dr. Pentland sent another letter to my GP when I left saying that I had "made good progress, with a notable improvement in cognitive function and an increase in insight". I was described as "fully cooperative" and Allan as "very sensible and supportive".

Over my time at this rehabilitation hospital, the main things that seemed to me to improve were my energy levels, my attention-span and my memory.

But much later I read the more detailed reports of my "considerable progress", and they were sobering.

My physiotherapist seemed reasonably content with my still (and evermore to be) bent and swollen finger – that was the good news.

The speech therapy report suggested that my retrograde amnesia was difficult to pinpoint time-wise but appeared to be New Year 1999, and therefore approximately two months before the injury. I now scored 100% in orientation and amnesia tests, and the Frenchay Aphasia Screening Test. The therapist noted, however, that although my verbal expression was at a high level, there was evidence of ongoing word-finding difficulties. I told her that I was usually able to substitute another suitable word. This was true. One can become quite adept at circumlocution. Nonetheless it erodes confidence. She went on to say that therapy tasks were pitched at a very high level, often taking the form of word puzzles. I was encouraged to complete crosswords in my own time.

My occupational therapist gave me pause for thought. Although I had scored adequately in all everyday simulations, the devil was in the detail. My "tactile discrimination" was reduced in my right hand. My times were slow for dexterity tasks and impaired for both right and left and for bilateral tasks. My upper left arm coordination was reduced. All in all, I tended to rush things "and not take the necessary care and attention to complete tasks successfully".

After an hour, said the therapist, I experienced fatigue. She was right, and I had no energy reserves now. Once I was tired, I had to sleep. My scores for cognitive tests were still described as "borderline" or "impaired". This embarrassed me when I first read it. My tendency to rush meant that I made mistakes. The initial contents of my written work were judged to have been "poor", with language errors, incorrect grammar, very long sentences and clumsy structure. I had the dimmest recollection now of being tested for this, but I do remember writing overlong sentences. Perhaps I was trying to impress, but failing. "These skills are all obviously important for her job," writes the therapist, "and I feel [her] speed of information processing is still slightly slow."

As a journalist, I had always prepared as meticulously as possible for interviews and reports, and I felt that I was good at absorbing new information fast and accurately. I would never have been seen as slapdash. Perhaps I was trying to behave the way I had always behaved, but without the brainpower I used to have.

Yet again, I was deemed to "lack insight into the extent of [my] difficulties and to make excuses for poor performance in tasks." Much later, I learned that this is called "confabulation" – telling tales – and is a regular consequence of brain injury. I was a typical offender.

The most humbling report came from the clinical psychologist. He did not mince his words.

Formal testing reveals significant cognitive impairments. Attention is generally very slow. Memory shows significant difficulties in both storage and recall of information over time, together with some interference. Both verbal and visual memory is similarly impaired, but verbal shows the more severe problems. There is moderate impairment of simple visual recognition. Complex visuo-spatial reasoning is severely impaired. Verbal reasoning is relatively impaired, being just in the "average" range. Verbal fluency is severely impaired for both lexical and semantic information. The demonstrated test difficulties are consistent with brain injury sustained, clearly emphasising the impaired frontal lobe functions.

He grudgingly added, "Her insight improved but there is some unrealistic expectation, at least for the short-term."

Most damningly, he closed with these words: "Her initial superficial presentation is generally very good and this may mislead others into thinking that her recovery is rather better than is the case so far."

Towards the end of my stay, the chief clinical psychologist called me in for a final assessment. At the end, he said, "We find improvement from the kind of injury you had to be much better if you're intelligent, and if you expect to improve. One of the biggest problems my patients typically have is drinking themselves to death in the pub." Then he told me about one of his other patients – a one-time professional ballroom dancer. She was now blind, and could neither talk nor walk. He shook his head.

I could understand why brain-injured people drink themselves to death. Recovery seemed to be so gradual (although I was being told that the professionals thought my progress was remarkable and unexpected). The temptation to lose heart must seduce a lot of sufferers into the easy oblivion of alcohol. I was determined not to fall victim to that risk. I felt that I must recover for my parents' sake, and Allan's. They had never been told how bleak my original prognosis was.

After three weeks as an in-patient at the Astley Ainslie in Edinburgh, I was discharged, into the care of Allan. Ten weeks spent in three hospitals had not achieved a full recovery, but I was able to live, with supervision, at home. I would continue to receive rehabilitation therapy as an outpatient.

Figure 5.2 Sheena and Allan leaving the Astley Ainslie Hospital, May 1999
Source: Andrew O'Brien, *Daily Mail*

I was warned before leaving the hospital that there was a photographer waiting outside. He was from the *Scotland on Sunday* newspaper. My hair was long and curly, and I was grinning manically, and showing off my fang – the front right incisor which had lost its crown. All that remained was the steel pin on which the crown was cemented. I looked like a crazed vampire.

Initially I did not go home, despite the relative success of the weekend home-visit. Allan worried that in these fragile early days, living on one level with no tiring flights of stairs would be easier. When friends of my family offered the use of a cottage in East Lothian, he accepted gratefully. The East Lothian cottage was near many good walks, and historical sites. Allan drove me around the county to visit these, and I introduced him to some of my childhood haunts. I was still very weak, needing hours of sleep every afternoon.

Figure 5.3 Sheena during her first year post-injury

Source: Stan Hunter, *Daily Mail*

The cottage in East Lothian was a godsend. Our days were structured very clearly. Rise late after a long sleep; breakfast; word games; something energetic in the morning – a walk into the village maybe, or a trip to a historic location; a long sleep in the afternoon; word games again; a TV show in the evening; early bed.

She had no difficulty coping with everyday activity at home except for suffering extreme fatigue – we walked about a mile, or mile and a half, and she found this very exhausting. It was also very disorientating for her to be outside in the city in crowds; she had continued blurred vision.

And I remained confused. Allan woke in the middle of the night to find me incompetently trying to climb out of the window in search of the bathroom.

I had never bothered with crossword puzzles before. They'd always seemed to me a waste of intellectual energy. But Sheena had been fiendishly good at The Times cryptic while she was at University and although she'd got out of the habit once she'd started working, I saw that this was something that we could do together, that would engage her mind, and give her problems to solve and – crucially – give her something she could teach me. I saw in it a way that she might improve the flexibility of her thinking.

Cryptic crosswords are a peculiarly British phenomenon; they're almost unknown in, say, France, where the purity of the language (compared to the mongrel nature of English) doesn't allow for punning and other forms of double meaning.

Here's how they work: take the clue "Lovely girl in crimson rose (8 letters)". This is a very straightforward cryptic clue. "Lovely girl" is "belle" and that word is, as indicated in the clue, contained with a word meaning crimson – "red". Insert the word "belle" into the word "red" and you get the answer – "REBELLED" – which means "rose", the last world of the clue.

The key to it is understanding that a word like "rose" can have not just more than one meaning; it can assume different parts of speech. In the clue it reads as a noun – a rose, or a flower. To get the answer you have to see past that and understand that it can also be an adjective (rose meaning "pink") or, in this case, the past tense of the verb "to rise". So this sense of "rose" is a synonym for "rebelled". I came to think of cryptic crosswords as a kind of work out for verbal dexterity. Sheena was learning again to put her brain through strenuous exercise and those exercises were encouraging her to flex and strengthen cognitive muscles that had been weakened by the injury or put out of action altogether.

This turned out to be great therapy. I found Sheena was able to sustain concentration over longer periods than she could when she was, say, reading a book. It forced her to think laterally about language and to search for words that were lodged somewhere in her head but had been made temporarily inaccessible by the injury.

For a short time we also played the children's game Boggle. *In this the players throw a set if dice that have letters of the alphabet rather than numbers on each side. You then give yourself two minutes to list as many words as you can from the available letters.*

And finally we played Scrabble. *These three games each engaged the verbal intellect and the cognitive powers in a slightly different way:* Boggle *for speed, cryptic crosswords for lateral thinking,* Scrabble *for concentration sustained over a long time. They were also ways that we could spend time together in a shared enterprise that was enjoyable as well as therapeutic and not physically demanding.*

Cognitive rehabilitation, recovery and brain plasticity

The introduction of these three word games by Allan was an intuitive stroke of genius! This reinforces that those closest to the patient often have the best solutions; this indeed was the best form of cognitive remediation, at this point in time. Why? First, the games provide structure and a focus for active thinking. As Sheena still had problems with attention, games that focus concentration in a specific way are helpful (and even better when they are enjoyable). As Sheena had enjoyed crosswords previously, and given her articulate and curious nature, word puzzles were the perfect choice. This is even more so when her future goal of returning to work as a journalist and interviewer is considered. Moreover, Sheena was still having word-finding difficulties and these word games target the retrieval of a specific and multiple words. The focus of the three tasks beautifully complement each other. As Allan had intuited, cryptic crosswords target lateral and abstract thinking, *Boggle* targets word generation from a prompt under speeded conditions (similar to neuropsychological word fluency tasks) and *Scrabble* targets both word knowledge and retrieval as well as sustained attention.

In 1999, Ian Robertson published a key piece of research on neurorehabilitation, brain plasticity and principles of guided recovery (Robertson and Murre, 1999). Crucially, the take-home message was that reconnection of damaged neural circuits is maximised by specific and guided behaviours. That is, potential for recovery depends on "providing precisely targeted bottom-up and top-down inputs, maintaining adequate levels of arousal, and avoiding activation of competitor circuits that may suppress activity in target circuits." (p. 544). The three word games undertaken by Sheena and Allan fulfil these requirements; namely, arousal (or concentration) is maintained through interaction and enjoyment, there is a clear goal of each game (top-down input) and there are precise bottom-up inputs for each item (e.g., the specific clue or set of letters). Since I listened to Ian Robertson talk about these principles, I have integrated and adapted these into my neurorehabilitation with many individuals (see what follows for further detail about other approaches to neurorehabilitation).

....

We attempted some little hikes – very little ones. Before the injury, it had been very easy indeed to walk round the immediate environs of the cottage. I now found the mile-long stroll more than enough. I felt ambitious enough to try climbing Berwick Law, normally an energetic half-hour scramble up a fairly steep but grass-tracked gradient. I fell – literally – at the second hurdle. As soon as the path started to climb, I lost my balance, and ended up in a giggling heap. Berwick Law would remain for the moment another long-term goal.

During our stay in East Lothian, Sheena's strength grew. Her memory was more retentive. She could cook, manage the house, and, with me at her side, go shopping. We even, once or twice, walked into the village to the local pub for lunch. She had the energy for one excursion a day, in the morning, and then slept in the afternoon.

But as normal social and domestic skills returned, there was also something that became clear to me only gradually: her mood, which had been very placid and benign since the injury, began to change and was growing more and more unpredictable.

I had always enjoyed the fact that I could make Sheena laugh easily. It had lit up our relationship; there was an easy, shared joy in it. But now she would laugh immoderately, sometimes making herself choke and splutter with the effort of it (her swallow was still unreliable).

She also, as time went on, became tearful and occasionally sullen. No-one had warned me that depression is often an after-effect of brain injury and it was only much later that I learned that this is what Sheena was slipping into.

I was now a regular outpatient at the Astley Ainslie, where physiotherapists, psychotherapists and an occupational therapist encouraged and challenged me. I also made regular visits to the dentist, for the reconstruction of the teeth that had been sheared off. Allan was determined that what defined "normal life" pre-injury should continue, as far as possible. We had taken a summer break for the previous two or three years on Cape Cod, Massachusetts, where we rented the house of a friend. In July 1999, Allan thought I would enjoy that. We spent three weeks on the Cape. I slept a lot, but had the energy for short walks in the woods.

I don't know why we went to Cape Cod in July. The stress of it was huge, not least the effort of trying to appear, for Sheena's sake, unstressed. But in the weeks beforehand, looking forward to revisiting the area we knew so well and had come to love had been great for morale.

Getting through the airport was grim. The queues for check-in long and slow, and I could see that just standing waiting was taking it out of Sheena. The crowded turmoil of the departure lounge, which Sheena would normally have taken in her stride, was also disorientating and tiring for her. As we waited I watched the energy drain out of her and silently willed the queue to move faster.

The house we had rented for several summer breaks before the injury was available again. Its familiarity was important to me. Sheena knew her way around it and that connected her in a new way to life before the injury. It had a beautiful garden overlooking a salt creek and was a short walk from local shops and restaurants. It was ideal.

Before the injury Sheena and I had filled our Cape Cod days with vigorous walks through woods, along cliff-tops and the length of the Great Atlantic Beach which runs for 40 miles. Sheena was keen to do this again.

It didn't take long to realise that this old way of spending our days on the Cape had gone. Those long adventurous walks were just not achievable. We tried though. Sheena complained that the insect life in the woods – the horse-flies and biting ticks that thrive there – was much worse than in previous years, that there must have been some change in the eco-system to account for this. The truth was that she was so much slower walking through insect-infested areas and was therefore a much easier target for the bugs. We gave up on the woods and opted instead to take an early morning dip in one of the lakes on the edge of our town.

But there was something else that was slowing Sheena down, in addition to the enduring fatigue. It was her weight.

By the time she was discharged from hospital she'd got very thin. At home she more than made up for this. She seemed permanently hungry, forever unable to satisfy her appetite. I didn't notice this at first, but she would, at almost every meal, help herself to a second portion of whatever was in the pot and then top that up by finishing whatever was left on my plate. For the first time in her life she developed a sweet tooth, sneaking sugary snacks between meals.

I began to worry about this, not least because Sheena didn't seem to realise what was happening. I began to feel quite isolated in my growing despair about it. One day, I watched one of Sheena's oldest friends tell her over and again how wonderful she was looking. I knew that she was doing this out of generosity; it was a kind and cheering thing to say. But the moment Sheena left the room that same friend turned to me and said, "My God Allan, you've got to get her to lose some weight."

"Thanks," I thought, but didn't say. "You've just reassured her that she looks wonderful." This would happen a lot in the months that lay ahead. I didn't know what to do about it. I was worried about Sheena's health, that the weight gain was self-perpetuating, in that the more she gained, the less inclined she was to do even mild exercise. It also dismayed me that her friends looked to me to "get her to lose some weight": there aren't many things that will undermine a relationship as effectively as a man repeatedly telling his partner that she is too fat. I knew that Sheena needed, more than anything, support from me, not criticism.

The holiday seemed to me to mark a turning-point, re-introducing me to relaxing without feeling like a patient, and allowing me to contemplate the liberty of more ambitious journeys. But the excessive and unnecessary eating continued, too. I gobbled chocolate as if it were nutritious.

I thought hard about what was causing this. The injury had clearly done something to her appetite control. But it was part of a wider behavioural pattern, aspects of which were becoming clearer to me. There was a tendency to seek immediate gratification. There was, for example, quite a lot of impulse buying. Internet shopping was in its infancy at this time, but Sheena took to it. Parcels would arrive at the house and Sheena would have forgotten that she'd ordered whatever was inside, and couldn't remember why she'd bought it or what she'd intended to do with it.

One day I came home to our house in London and, on the kitchen table, there was an enormous box of fresh fish – enough, probably, for a dozen meals at least. "It was a bargain," Sheena said, "A van came down the street selling it. It's absolutely fresh! Straight out of the sea.

*It only cost £200. You'd pay far more than that at Tesco." She seemed
pleased with this and I think expected me to be enthusiastic too.*

*We didn't have a freezer. And even if we did have a freezer, I rea-
soned, putting it in there would mean it was no longer fresh. I tried
to be supportive, as we jammed as much as we could into the little
ice-box in our fridge, and threw much of the rest of it away when it
began to turn.*

*Years later, when Sheena was pretty much fully recovered and we
could talk about these things with greater detachment, she and I went
to visit a group of brain-injury survivors at a rehabilitation centre in
Glasgow. Sheena was well-known in Scotland from her TV days and the
people there, each differently affected by their injury, were all delighted
to see her and, I think, felt pleased that she had been just like them and
had done so well. I told the story about the fish. A woman in the group
laughed and said "That's funny. I bought three new kitchens on the
phone! My husband had to ring up and cancel them all!"*

*I learned that there is a whole body of research into the psychol-
ogy of impulse buying: that it satisfies a need in us that evolution
bequeathed; that it may be associated with a disordered or a disrupted lifestyle. You don't have to have had a bang on the head to be
susceptible to impulse buying: I have had a problem with book-buy-
ing most of my life and have accrued far more books than I can ever
hope to read, but that doesn't stop me buying new ones. The more I
thought about this the more I came to understand that the behavioural
changes I could see in Sheena were extreme examples of normal, non-
brain-injured human experience.*

*The challenge as I saw it was to try to encourage Sheena to under-
stand her own behaviour, and to change it.*

*I would learn, too, that lack of self-knowledge is a common side-effect
of brain injury – an inability to properly assess one's own behaviour, or to
judge what is, or is not, appropriate behaviour in any given context. This
can manifest itself as an extreme form of "disinhibition", in which the
brain-injury survivor shows a lack of normal restraint, behaves aggres-
sively, or manically, or causes offence by failing to judge that what they
are saying is rude or hurtful. At its worst it can result, especially in men,
in sexually inappropriate behaviour in public as well as private.*

*Disinhibition is often associated, after brain injury, with injury to the
frontal lobes; Sheena had suffered injury to the right frontal lobe when
the police van had hit her immediately above the right eye.*

*I began to see that she was mildly disinhibited, in the sense that – and
especially when she was tired – she had lost the ability to monitor her own
behaviour. I came home one day to find her on the phone having quite an*

animated and friendly conversation. She was going through her diary, explaining in great detail what she had coming up in the days ahead.

On Tuesday there's an exhibition at such-and-such a gallery. I'll go to that in the morning. My mother's coming for tea in the afternoon so I'll have to be back by 3 p.m., and that'll give me time to pop to the shops to get what I need for that . . .

and on and on through the days. When, after ten minutes or so, the call ended, I asked her who it was on the other end. To my astonishment she said it was the plumber: she'd been trying to find a suitable time for him to come and fix a leaky tap.

"Why were you telling him in great detail all your social engagements for the next two weeks?" I asked. "I wasn't. I was only trying to find a time when I knew I'd be here to let him in."

It was harmless enough, I suppose. But it wasn't normal behaviour. The key, again, was to find a way to encourage her to understand this.

In these early months there was also a lot of what I came to call "tangential talking". In conversation with friends Sheena would start to contribute to the conversation and in the course of talking she would say something that would trigger another thought altogether. She would then abruptly change the subject and go down another track, which in turn would lead to another new thought and another new track. This again is harmless in its way, but it also made sequential conversation impossible, and Sheena would often seem completely unaware that she had been talking non-stop for 15 or 20 minutes with no-one else adding to the conversation at all. This, unchecked, would make normal social life very difficult, and regaining a normal social life I thought of as a key to the return to a liveable, fulfilled life.

After the holiday, we moved back to my flat in the centre of Edinburgh, but the circumference of my world remained tiny. Whereas in my working life I had always been very interested in national and international events and affairs, I was now interested in my immediate surroundings. And my powers of self-assessment remained severely compromised. Day and daily, I thought I was doing better and better. In fact I was merely inching towards approximate normality, at a near-imperceptible pace – and ever-increasing girth. Having lost so much weight when I was in three hospitals, I now over-compensated by eating to excess. The weight quickly piled on. I have seen nothing relating to this in the clinical volumes I have read but wonder whether the original injury had paralysed whatever mechanism controls appetite.

Frontal "executive" functions: the subtleties of disinhibition

As initiation increases, *impulses and disinhibition* can become more prominent. The balance between initiation and inhibition is finely tuned. What Allan describes are manifestations of faulty inhibition processes, which is a process associated with the right lateral frontal lobe (for a review see Aron et al., 2014). As a clinician, I have seen disinhibition manifest in various forms including tangential speech (Barker et al., 2017), jocular and rhyming speech (Robinson and Ceslis, 2014) and "pressure" of speech where a patient could not stop talking (Robinson et al., 2015a). My colleagues and I found that patients with very focal damage to the right frontal lobe were associated with verbal disinhibition and also not applying a strategy to overcome this (Robinson et al., 2015b). I will return to this study when I discuss Sheena's reassessment as it was key in understanding her behaviours.

With respect to impulsive eating and buying, there is a growing body of research from patients with frontotemporal dementia (FTD) that provides important clues. FTD is characterised by a greater degree of neurodegeneration in the frontal and temporal lobes, in both the left and right hemispheres. There are several forms of FTD, one being the "behavioural variant" (bvFTD) that disproportionately affects the frontal lobe and results in overeating and developing a preference for sweet foods. Recent studies have found that eating abnormalities are partly related to hypothalamic degeneration and potential decreases in the connection between the hypothalamus and the orbitofrontal region (Ahmed et al., 2015). In addition to hypothalamus involvement, the prefrontal cortex has been implicated in metabolism and eating regulation (van der Klaauw and Farooqi, 2015).

While we cannot be sure about the integrity of Sheena's hypothalamus and connection to the orbitofrontal region, the latter area is adjacent to the right inferior frontal lobe and these regions are located at the base of the frontal lobe next to the skull. These are regions frequently damaged in TBIs. For Sheena, we have indications that this area was damaged as (1) her sense of smell was poorer (the olfactory bulbs similarly are located at the base of the frontal brain region along the skull) and (2) she experienced temperature regulation changes (related to hypothalamus control). Although supposition at this point, it is likely that the combination of right inferior frontal and hypothalamus damage combined to give rise to increased eating and the weight gain. Clinically, this was one of the most challenging aspects of Sheena's ongoing neurorehabilitation.

When we moved back to our home in Edinburgh, things got worse. Gradually, I was beginning to go back to work. Sheena seemed to take my absences as a personal slight. I tried to reason, arguing that I had to work, that the only alternative to going back to work was to resign and lose my livelihood; how would we then live? Sheena was coming to resent my work, my colleagues and even the employer that had kept me on the books through the long absence of the early months of her recovery.

For a long time after the injury, Sheena's world was much diminished. She was the centre of that reduced world. She resented anything that disordered it, or intruded on it. This included my work. She seemed to think it was selfish of me to go to work, that it proved I cared more about the BBC than about her. I would leave the house with a knot in my stomach, knowing that I faced a gruelling day in a high powered job, and at the end of it not know what kind of reception I would come home to. Which Sheena would be there at the end of the day – the gentle, funny, laughing carefree one, or the angry sullen one?

One more useful by-product of my altered state was that I did not suffer too much when Allan was away. As the months passed, I was deemed able to look after myself without supervision. One of the signs of getting back to quasi-normal would be my adverse reaction to hearing he was off again!

Seven months after Sheena's injury, I had my first weekend off since her injury. It was the first time I had been away from Sheena since the day after she had been run over. I had had a long-standing arrangement to go to Sarajevo with my oldest friend, Alan. He and I had gone there in our teens while backpacking round Europe in our student summer holidays. We'd promised ourselves a return visit to mark the 20th anniversary of that trip.

I tried to enjoy it. I was trying to demonstrate even to him, my closest friend, that nothing had changed, that everything was going back to normal. I was only away for 48 hours but throughout the trip I was constantly worrying about how Sheena was. I had no mobile phone then and no email contact. I tried calling from public phones a couple of times but there was no answer. When I got back, late on Sunday evening, I found Sheena sitting in our living room alone, in the dark. I turned the light on. She told me to turn it off – that it hurt her eyes. She behaved as though I were a complete stranger, was barely able to talk to me. "I'm sorry I've been away. I tried to call," I said. "Don't worry about it," she said and there was an icy detachment and a terrifying dark desolation in her tone. "My mother said a leopard never changes its spots. She's right."

I think this is what the principal carer of the brain-injury survivor has to be ready for – you will be blamed at work and you will be blamed at home.

Everyone will ask after your partner, say how delighted they are about how well he or she is doing, how brave she is, how positive, how determined, even how cheerful she is despite everything. And when everyone else has gone, and you are alone, you will be the only one left to take the full force of the resentment and frustration and sense of betrayal that brain-injury leaves in its wake. You will be made to feel unwelcome in your own home. It is hard not to slip into self-pity – though I could see that that was, in a sense, what Sheena was now doing. It is hard not to answer like with like, hard not to bite back, hard to keep reminding yourself that this is the injury talking and not the person you love. You feel put upon, unfairly judged. "My mother says a leopard never changes its spots."

One evening we were out for drinks with friends who had known Sheena for 20 years or more. We were in a bar somewhere in the West End of London. It was early evening and fairly quiet. They were asking Sheena how she'd been. Sheena had learned to talk about her progress, her ongoing treatment, the prospect maybe of finding work again – in other words of giving the impression that everything was getting back to normal. And then suddenly James, whom I hardly knew at the time but who would in the years ahead become one of my closest friends, turned to me and said "And what about you? Who's looking after you?"

It struck me then that this was an unfamiliar question precisely because no-one had thought to ask it before. It hit me like a train. I shook my head and tried to change the subject but I couldn't speak. I walked away and fat tears rolled down my face and I had to suppress a throaty sob that rose from somewhere deep down.

You get emotionally ambushed like this by small acts of kindness or expressions of concern. One day I was picking up dry-cleaning. Behind the counter was a courteous but taciturn older man in a beard and turban. A younger man I took to be his son sat in the window mending clothes. There was a picture of a great mosque lit up at night on the wall behind him. Sheena and I had used this dry-cleaner often before the injury but I had seldom exchanged more than a few words with two men I'd assumed were conservative, reserved, religiously observant. I pushed a £20 note across the counter and the older man quietly pushed it back at me and said, shyly, "No. I read about your lovely wife. Please take the money and buy her some flowers."

I thanked him, left his shop and knew I was falling apart a bit. I bought flowers and walked home. I gave the flowers to Sheena but couldn't get the words out to explain where they had come from. I sat on the couch and cried uncontrollably for about 15 minutes. I think it was the first time that Sheena got some sense of the extent to which this whole experience was grinding me down.

Formally, I was still under the supervision of the National Hospital for Neurology and Neurosurgery in London.

In August, Gail Robinson produced another neuropsychological report based on a fresh assessment, which concluded that I was now "functioning in the superior range on the verbal scale and in the very superior range on the performance scale of the WAIS-R . . . the main difficulty remaining is fatigue and the impact of this on cognitive functioning."

Neuropsychological reassessment: the devil is in the detail

When Sheena returned to London, my first task was to review her progress by completing a neuropsychological reassessment. It had only been five months since I last saw her. How much recovery from a very severe TBI can really occur in that time? Well, I was stunned! This was a different person. To start, she was no longer confused. She completed test after test rapidly and at a high level that it is rare, let alone for someone only six months post-TBI (see Table 5.1).

Table 5.1 Sheena's neuropsychological assessments, March and
August 1999

COGNITIVE DOMAINS Tests	12 March 1999 (14 days post-TBI)	19 August 1999 (~ six months post-TBI)
		Range (score: percentile)
PREMORBID INTELLECTUAL FUNCTIONING		
NART Equivalent IQ[1]	Superior (120: 90th percentile)	-
INTELLECTUAL FUNCTIONS		
WAIS-R Verbal IQ[2]	Borderline (75: <10th percentile)	Superior (129: >90th percentile)
WAIS-R Performance IQ[2]	-	Very superior (140: >95th percentile)
Advanced Progressive Matrices[3]	Average (7/12: 50–75th percentile)	Superior (12/12: >90th percentile)

MEMORY

Orientation to person, place and time	PTA (disoriented)	Oriented
Recognition memory test: words[4]	Poor (21/25: short version)	Superior (49/50: >90th percentile)
Recognition memory test: faces[4]	-	High average (47/50: 75–90th percentile)
Recall memory: AMIPB Stories[5]	-	Superior (>90th percentile)
Recall memory: Rey complex figure[6]	-	Average (50–75th percentile)

LANGUAGE AND NUMERACY FUNCTIONS

Graded Naming Test: objects[7]	Impaired (3/30: <5th percentile)	Superior (27/30: <90th percentile)
Proper nouns	-	Superior (27/30: <90th percentile)
Reading (NART)[1]	Superior (41/50: 90th percentile)	-
Spelling[8]	-	Superior (28/30: >90th percentile)
Arithmetic[9]	-	High Average (16/24: 75-90th percentile)

VISUAL PERCEPTION/SPATIAL

Incomplete letters test (VOSP)[10]	Intact (19/20)	-
Object decision test (VOSP)[10]	-	Intact (20/20)

FRONTAL EXECUTIVE

Similarities (WAIS-R)[2]	Borderline impaired *Concrete responses* (<10th percentile)	Superior *Abstract responses* (>90th percentile)
Colour Form Sorting: Weigl Test[11]	Pass (2/2)	-
Modified Card Sorting Test[12]	-	Pass (6/6)

(continued)

Table 5.1   (continued)

COGNITIVE DOMAINS Tests	12 March 1999 (14 days post-TBI)	19 August 1999 (~ six months post-TBI)
		Range (score: percentile)
Word fluency: "s"[13]	-	High average (21 words: 75–90th percentile)
Trails B[14]	-	Satisfactory with no errors
Cognitive estimates[15]	Poor	-
Hayling Sentence Completion Test[16]	-	Average–Low average
SPEED OF PROCESSING		
Number cancellation[17]	Slow with many errors	-
AMIPB Speed of processing[5]	-	Superior (>90th percentile)

Notes: 1 Nelson and Willison (1991); 2 Wechsler (1981); 3 Raven (1990); 4 Warrington (1984); 5 Coughlan and Hollows (1985); 6 Rey (1941) 7 Warrington (1997); 8 Baxter and Warrington (1994); 9 Jackson and Warrington (1986); 10 Warrington and James (1991); 11 Weigl (1941); 12 Nelson (1976); 13 Benton (1968); 14 Reitan and Wolfson (1985); 15 Shallice and Evans (1978); 16 Burgess and Shallice (1997); 17 Willison and Warrington (1992).

Sheena performed well above that of most people on almost every single test that I chose. Is this possible? Had I not chosen tests that assess a crucial ability? I have no doubt that on most traditional neuropsychological tests, Sheena would have passed with flying colours. A neuropsychological assessment helps me to predict what might be problematic when a patient is faced with everyday life situations and tasks. Well, the clues for Sheena were in the assessment. When I read my own conclusion, there it is. Yes, slightly buried and in my cautious "soft" language as I know that my reports are a permanent record that a patient is likely to read. And here we are almost 20 years on doing just that! This is what I concluded: "Her performance on tests of frontal lobe function was primarily adequate except for a mild inefficiency on one test . . . The main difficulty remaining is fatigue and the impact of this on cognitive function." The mild inefficiency was on the Hayling Sentence Completion Test that assesses verbal initiation, inhibition and strategy use. This finding influenced the direction I took in the weeks and months that followed, along with prominent fatigue, and became the foundation of our initial period of outpatient rehabilitation. In the next chapter I will return to the specific goals and focus of this long period of neurorehabilitation.

My approach to neurorehabilitation

When I started to work with Sheena and Allan in 1999, I was influenced by cognitive, behavioural, experimental and holistic neuropsychological rehabilitation approaches. There were a number of prominent individuals and centres around the world including Barbara Wilson and the Oliver Zangwill Centre (UK), Anne-Lise Christensen at Copenhagen (Denmark), and then Yehuda Ben Yishay at New York University and George Prigatano in Phoenix, Arizona (USA). McKay Sohlberg and Catherine Mateer also proposed a helpful set of general practice principles for cognitive rehabilitation (summarised by Mateer, 2005):

1 Cognitive interventions must be tailored to the individual.
2 Cognitive interventions are most effectively viewed as a collaboration between the client, the client's family or caregivers, and the therapist.
3 Cognitive intervention should be focused on mutually set and functionally relevant goals.
4 Evaluation of efficacy and outcome should incorporate and capture changes in functional abilities.
5 Most successful cognitive interventions are eclectic and involve multiple approaches.
6 Interventions should address the affective and emotional components of cognitive loss or inefficiency.
7 Interventions should be self-evaluative.

These principles become more prominent as neurorehabilitation progresses beyond the acute and post-acute stages. In Sheena's case, they guided my work over the next five years.

BINJ clinic

In 1999, Dr. Richard Greenwood and I started an outpatient brain injury clinic, which became known as the "BINJ" clinic, at the National Hospital. This was a triage clinic where patients who had sustained an acquired brain injury of any kind attended for a neurological consultation, a neuro-psychology assessment and a brain MRI, followed by a consultation to plan further neurorehabilitation. It was designed for individuals like Sheena who were walking and talking, but needed specific input in order to return to previous life roles, be they vocational or psychosocial.

The main follow-up intervention was neuropsychological rehabilitation, which is how Sheena and Allan came to see me regularly but spaced out over a five-year period. My experience in the BINJ clinic, with many individuals similar to Sheena, is that *low intensity* input over a *longer period of time* is key to successful outcomes. This means input at times of transition or change or for specific goals as problems arise, rather than what is often available, which is multiple sessions within a short defined time (e.g., three months). This allows for progression of goals and gradual change over time, which is the nature of recovery from severe-TBI.

The BINJ clinic is unique and I was fortunate that my Head of Neuropsychology at the National Hospital, Lisa Cipolotti, supported a service that offered low intensity input over a long period of time as the optimal form for outpatient neuropsychological rehabilitation. This was not an intentional decision, but rather this model of service evolved as it became clear that this is what individuals like Sheena needed.

....

In October I attended a follow-up appointment with the consultant neu-rologist in London, Richard Greenwood. He was to give me the results of my most recent set of tests, all diagnostic, all trying to establish the degree to which my brain was injured.

I had improved. In a test on the day, I mistook Abraham Lincoln for D.H. Lawrence – but I had never met either of them . . . Dr. Greenwood shook his head. "You've broken the rules," he said. "We didn't expect you to recover all your cognitive and motor functions, and certainly not so fast." "So how have I?" I asked.

"You tell us."

Gail and Dr. Greenwood admitted astonishment. Looking at the results of a new brain scan and at the series of cognitive tests that Sheena had undergone, she was scoring "at ceiling level" – in other words maxi-mum possible performance. It shouldn't really have happened, we are told – and certainly not so quickly.

I was cock-a-hoop after my London assessment, and so bound to come down with a bang.

That happened a month later, in November 1999, when I had my eyes inspected and was told my sight was permanently damaged, and I would not be able to drive any more. Allan was out of the country. I had to wait for over an hour before being examined, and the ophthalmologist was brusque and business-like.

You've had bad luck. You've damaged your occipital lobe, and lost your right field vision in both eyes. You'd have been better off if you'd lost the sight of one eye, but as it is, we don't recommend that you drive any more.

I tried to get used to the idea of not driving again. Ever. Sometimes I allowed myself to remember driving trips I had done in the past. From Albuquerque to Santa Fe, from Santa Fe to Bandelier National Park, an awesome, craggy landscape, then down to Carlsbad Caverns, home to tens of thousands of bats. From Johannesburg to KwaZulu-Natal, following a punishing schedule for Channel 4 News, after selling them the idea of a film on how that country was beginning to change since the abandonment of apartheid. From Edinburgh to Cardiff, from Edinburgh to Leeds, from Edinburgh to the Isle of Skye, again and again. It had become as natural a life-skill as singing or reading.

And now I had to cross it out, as my own name had been crossed out of potential employers' contact-books less than a year before. After the initial thrill of surviving against the odds had worn off, there began the long, slow grind of regaining work and reputation, of convincing the sceptical that brain-injury is not necessarily a permanently disabling state, if for no other reason than that I have no wish to end up on the streets for lack of income.

The Driver and Vehicle Licensing Agency (DVLA) now requested that I have a further eye test. Allan was in Zimbabwe, so I left home for the optician with no encouraging hug. I felt apprehensive and pessimistic. The optician put me through my paces, asking me to focus on one light, and squeeze a button every time I saw another.

Even if I had been tempted to cheat, it was impossible in these tests. I gazed at the light, and began.

After I had completed the test, the optician declared herself satisfied.

"Well, that's fine," she said.

"I've passed?" I squeaked, disbelieving.

"Yes – I'll send this form on to the DVLA."

I was flabbergasted. I had just experienced another miracle. Either the DVLA standards are dangerously low – which I doubt – or my chance-in-a-million of improving my eyesight was taking place. My first reaction was to want another brain scan, to see whether the empty void in the region of my occipital lobe had somehow regenerated – although I knew that was impossible. Brain cells, once destroyed, cannot restore themselves. So had another part of my brain taken on the functions of the damaged part? I had not thought that eyesight was a transferable function. All would have to wait until my next medical eye test with the ophthalmologist at the National Hospital, which would be monocular, rather than the binocular test which the DVLA stipulates.

The result was compared with the original one, and showed slight improvement. How? "The occipital lobe was clearly severely traumatised," said the ophthalmologist. When he tested me again, six months later, he saw further improvement. So what did the black hole in the original brain-scan signify? Gail had a suggestion:

"If you retained a little part of that," she said, "the remaining fragment may take on all the functions previously carried out by the full lobe."

What a fabulous and mysterious organ the brain is.

References

Ahmed, R.M., Latheef, S., Bartley, L., Irish, M., Halliday, G.M., Kiernan, M.C., Hodges, J.R. and Piguet, O. (2015). "Eating behavior in frontotemporal dementia". *Neurology*, 85(15), 1310–1317.

Aron, A.R., Robbins, T.W. and Poldrack, R.A. (2014). "Inhibition and the right inferior frontal cortex: one decade on". *Trends in Cognitive Sciences*, 18(4), 177–185.

Barker, M.S., Young, B. and Robinson, G.A. (2017). "Cohesive and coherent connected speech deficits in mild stroke". *Brain and Language*, 168, 23–36.

Baxter, D.M. and Warrington, E.K. (1994). "Measuring dysgraphia: a graded-difficulty spelling test". *Behavioural Neurology*, 7(3–4), 107–116.

Benton, A. (1968). "Differential behavioural effects in frontal lobe disease". *Neuropsychologia*, 6, 53–60.

Burgess, P. and Shallice, T. (1997). *The Hayling and Brixton Tests: Test Manual.* London: Thames Valley Test Company.

Coughlan, A.K. and Hollows, S.E. (1985). *The Adult Memory and Information Processing Battery (AMIPB): Test Manual.* Leeds: A.K. Coughlan, Psychology Department, St James' University Hospital.

Jackson, M. and Warrington, E.K. (1986). "Arithmetic skills in patients with unilateral cerebral lesions". *Cortex*, 22(4), 611–620.

Mateer, C.A. (2005). *Fundamentals of Cognitive Rehabilitation.* New York, NY: Oxford University Press.

Nelson, H.E. (1976). "A modified card sorting test sensitive to frontal lobe defects". *Cortex*, 12(4), 313–324.

Nelson, H. and Willison, J. (1991). *The National Adult Reading Test*, 2nd edition. Windsor: The NFER-Nelson Publishing Co. Ltd.

Raven, J. (1990). *Advanced Progressive Matrices Sets I and II*. Oxford: Oxford Psychologists Press Ltd.

Reitan, R.M. and Wolfson, D. (1985). *The Halstead-Reitan Neuropsychological Test Battery: Theory and Clinical Interpretation*, Vol. 4. Tucson, AZ: Neuropsychology Press.

Rey, A. (1941). "L'examen psychologique dans les cas d'encéphalopathie traumatique (Les problems)". *Archives de psychologie*, 28, 215–285.

Robertson, I.H. and Murre, J.M. (1999). "Rehabilitation of brain damage: brain plasticity and principles of guided recovery". *Psychological Bulletin*, 125(5), 544.

Robinson, G. and Ceslis, A. (2014). "An unusual presentation of probable dementia: rhyming, associations, and verbal disinhibition". *Journal of Neuropsychology*, 8(2), 289–294.

Robinson, G.A., Butterworth, B. and Cipolotti, L. (2015a). "'My mind is doing it all': no 'brake' to stop speech generation in jargon aphasia". *Cognitive and Behavioral Neurology*, 28(4), 229–241.

Robinson, G.A., Cipolotti, L., Walker, D.G., Biggs, V., Bozzali, M. and Shallice, T. (2015b). "Verbal suppression and strategy use: a role for the right lateral prefrontal cortex?". *Brain*, 138(4), 1084–1096.

Shallice, T. and Evans, M.E. (1978). "The involvement of the frontal lobes in cognitive estimation". *Cortex*, 14(2), 294–303.

van der Klaauw, A.A. and Farooqi, I.S. (2015). "The hunger genes: pathways to obesity". *Cell*, 161(1), 119–132.

Warrington, E.K. (1984). *The Recognition Memory Test*. East Sussex: NFER-Nelson Publishing Company.

Warrington, E. (1997)." The Graded Naming Test: a restandardisation". *Neuropsychological Rehabilitation*, 7, 143–146.

Warrington, E. and James, M. (1991). *Visual Object and Space Perception Battery*. London: Thames Valley Test Company.

Wechsler, D. (1981). *Wechsler Adult Intelligence Scale-Revised*. San Antonio, TX: The Psychological Corporation.

Weigl, E. (1941). "On the psychology of so-called processes of abstraction". *Journal of Normal and Social Psychology*, 36, 3–33.

Willison, J.R. and Warrington, E.K. (1992). "Cognitive retardation in a patient with preservation of psychomotor speed". *Behavioural Neurology*, 5(2), 113–116.

Wilson, B.A. and Gracey, F. (2009). "Towards a comprehensive model of neuropsychological rehabilitation". Chapter 1 in B.A Wilson, F. Gracey, J.J. Evans and A. Bateman (eds), *Neuropsychological Rehabilitation: Theory, Models, Therapy and Outcome* (pp. 1–21). Cambridge: Cambridge University Press.

Chapter 6

Back to work

The first piece of work that I did after the injury was commissioned by the photographer Eve Arnold, who had been a kind friend throughout my recovery. She had planned an exhibition of photographs taken by the five woman members (including herself) of the photographic agency, Magnum. The show was called Magna Brava, and was to be displayed at the Scottish National Portrait Gallery, nine months after my injury. Photographs are in many ways a portrait of the photographer, and one learns a lot about the best – Imogen Cunningham, Henri Cartier-Bresson, Lee Miller, André Kertész, Eve Arnold herself – by looking at the work they have created.

Eve had mooted this idea before my injury, and had asked whether I might write one of the forewords, along with Isabella Rossellini and Christiane Amanpour, to the coffee-table book which would accompany this show. Once she considered I was able to make sense again, she phoned: will you still be able to do this? Yes, I said. I was determined, and managed to tap out what I think about photography as an art-form, and as a form of journalism.

I sent my effort off to Eve with some foreboding. She did not ever suffer fools gladly, and I wondered if I had submitted foolish convalescent musings. She called back, and offered me one of the greatest compliments I have received in my life.

"It's fine."

The show was wonderful, and the book beautifully published. Eve then asked me to chair a historic gathering in St Andrews, bringing together the women photographers and their fans. The event went well – and I felt that I was "back on the bike", in a world of aspiration and skill.

Neuropsychological rehabilitation and community integration

After an individual is discharged from post-acute neurorehabilitation it is a process of expanding focus and resuming life roles in whatever form this takes; that is, integrating back into the community. This focus and approach maximises an individual's quality of life and, consequently, functional outcomes (Ritchie et al., 2014). Outpatient neuropsychological rehabilitation comprises a series of sessions in which the goal or focus is identified and then addressed. In each session, I first set the agenda based on our overall goal and in consultation at the start of each session with the individual. At the end of each session I identify specific actions to be the focus before the next session. Developing agreed-upon goals, agendas and actions are crucial for both therapist and client. As an aside, I still use the term "patient" rather than "client" as individuals associate me with attending sessions at a hospital. It can be confusing to be known as a client or even worse, consumer! "Patient" is not ambiguous and it depends entirely on how you interact with an individual as to whether they feel terminology is a priority issue. As for Sheena, when she attended as an outpatient more than six months post-TBI, she was not a patient or client: she was simply Sheena.

Neuropsychological rehabilitation and Sheena

What was the focus?

There were several main themes running throughout the five years, with some progression, as follows:

1   *Frontal lobe functions* – planning and organisation with strategies to follow through and overcome impulsiveness; social awareness and judgement.

2   *Fatigue* – management with diary to create a routine with planned breaks and naps. This decreased with time, and ceased when the case was settled in October 2002.

3   *Weight* – regulation of food intake and exercising was an ongoing issue.

4   *Mood* – depression and grief, which presented about one year post-TBI.

5   *Identity and sense of self* – adjustment to loss and new sense of self.

6   *Relationship with Allan* – ongoing and shifting from carer to partner.

Frontal lobe functions and returning to work

First, in mid-October 1999 and directly stemming from the neuropsychological reassessment in August, I wanted to ensure that I had fully assessed Sheena's nominal language and executive functions. I gave her a few select tests as follows:

- Brixton Spatial Anticipation Test, a nonverbal test of reasoning (High Average).
- Verbal Switching Task, a word flexibility task that requires the generation of as many meanings of a word as possible (e.g., tick; Sheena scored very high).
- Stroop Test of inhibition of automatic responses (no errors and fast).
- Category Naming Test to assess naming of low frequency items from four different categories (animals, fruits/vegetables, praxic objects, nonpraxic objects). Sheena was almost flawless on this test (25 or above/30).

Second, I gathered detailed information about her work as a broadcast journalist so that I could map any subtle deficits onto this in order to predict and plan for potential pitfalls. The four additional tests I gave Sheena were related to word demands and cognitive difficulties. Specifically, retrieving words at speed and flexibly shifting between ideas was crucial; hence, the difficult category naming and verbal switching tasks. The Brixton is a complex task that requires inductive reasoning, in other words problem solving, which is crucial when faced with new challenging situations. Finally, given the mild inhibition difficulties on the Hayling Sentence Completion Test I gave Sheena the Stroop Test for corroboration.

Third, we discussed strategies for expressive language fluency as Sheena had already committed to chairing several public engagements. In addition, strategies included managing fatigue as this was considerable and unpredictable.

....

Obviously I couldn't take up my old post in Moscow. The BBC advertised this job and replaced me. I had to find something in London so that Sheena and I could live in Sheena's house there. To my relief one of the best film-makers in the BBC's Current Affairs department asked me to work with him on a project that would take seven or eight months to complete – a so-called "landmark" two-hour long documentary for BBC

Two on NATO's intervention in Kosovo, which had taken place earlier that year. I knew former Yugoslavia well: I'd spent four years there in the early 1990s during the wars in Croatia and Bosnia. I'd missed this latest phase of the country's tragedy because it had taken place in the weeks after Sheena's injury and I had barely had the time or energy to watch, never mind report, the news. It seemed ideal: a project on a subject I knew well that would keep me in London for the rest of that year and well into the following. That would enable me to be at home while Sheena's recovery progressed.

It turned out not to be the lifeline I'd been hoping for. The programme's producer was, indeed, one of the most talented rising stars at the BBC, very highly regarded by his bosses as well as many of those who worked for him. But he was also a ferocious workaholic, often starting work at 9 a.m., staying all day, all evening, spending all night in an edit suite and then working right through the following day before going home exhausted after 36 hours in the office. I could not have kept pace with this in normal circumstances. And these were not normal circumstances.

I cared about my professional reputation. I tried to behave normally. It was a mistake. I think I was still trying to "return to normal". I had not yet understood what "no going back to the way things were" really meant. I regret now that the opportunity to work with this talented man did not work out happily. But I also see, in retrospect, that it is probably the only time in my working life that I allowed myself to be bullied. The talented ambitious young man in charge of the project hadn't the slightest notion or concern about what was happening in my world: why should he be bothered about that? He just wanted me to give my professional best: it's why he'd taken me on. In the two weeks before Christmas he sent me to the United States, three times, each time on day trips – twice to Washington, D.C. and once to New York. The trans-Atlantic flights were punishing – an early morning flight from Heathrow, a taxi into town, a long, demanding and detailed TV interview in the early afternoon (one of them was with Madeleine Albright, then still in office as Secretary of State) then back to the airport, an overnight flight back to Heathrow (in economy class, naturally) and back into the office to go through the interview. Then the same thing a few days later, and again a few days after that. Trying to keep pace with the demands of my job was grinding me down. I now profoundly regret caving into these requests, for it left me in no fit state to give Sheena the attention she still needed.

I was losing control. I was exhausted. I was trying to behave at work as though everything was fine. One day, in an effort to close the widening gap between me and the programme's editor, I asked him, quietly, whether everything was OK. "No," he said. "I think you are hiding behind Sheena's illness, using it as an excuse not to pull your weight." I listened in stunned silence, without the energy or the inclination to defend myself.

I was inching forward. My first broadcast-work target was in Durban, where I had been hired, pre-injury, to present an edition of *International Question Time* (a BBC World Service phone-in programme which I had anchored for several years) with foreign ministers from five Commonwealth countries. Allan asked the BBC to break its own rules and fly me – and him – down to South Africa in business class; normally economy class is what is expected even for long haul overnight flights. They agreed. Robin Cook took part, along with four of his Commonwealth peers – and all performed as hoped for, this time in front of an invited and very animated local audience.

Back in Britain, I gave Gail a recording of the programme. She listened and was surprised.

"I didn't think you'd manage that," she said, "but, of course, I didn't tell you."

I was glad. Retaining confidence is one of the key elements to recovery, I'm told, and I believe it.

At the end of 1999, Sheena flew to South Africa to chair a very public and high profile meeting. I thought it was too soon, yet I had had no concrete evidence or reason to presume she would fail or to equivocally say that it was a bad idea. This is why I had quickly implemented strategies to manage the cognitive "inefficiencies". Sometimes as clinicians all we can do is prepare for the worst and hope for the best. Sheena was determined to attempt these work engagements and I am sure this quality in part drove her recovery.

Yes, Sheena's performance was excellent and I was certainly relieved! There is a fine balance between providing feedback about problems to work on and improvements then achievements to celebrate. Sheena had cognitive inefficiencies that were quickly impacted by fatigue. The key here was to pro-actively and vigilantly manage her fatigue to minimise the impact on thinking. A big unknown was also how she would respond to an international flight. As I indicated previously, my approach is to trouble-shoot and plan for all the potential pitfalls and then hope that none occur or that the strategies to manage are sufficient. Retaining confidence is very important, especially early in the process. Neurorehabilitation typically involves attempting tasks that increase in difficulty to build confidence. However, we usually start with the small easy tasks rather than a live international broadcast!

Did I recall the Edinburgh psychiatrist's assessment six months previously? – "Her initial superficial presentation is generally very good and this may mislead others into thinking that her recovery is rather better than is the case so far." I had not read his words at this stage; I simply thought that I seemed to have got away with it.

I went on to prepare for my first British public engagement since the injury – the one I had agreed to do when in hospital, very soon after regaining a form of consciousness: presenting the Gramophone Awards before an audience of 2,000 in London's Royal Festival Hall. These are the premier annual awards for what is judged the best CD recording of a piece of classical music, in various categories, of that year. I had presented the ceremony the previous year, and was determined to be well enough to do it again this year. In retrospect, I wonder about the power of denial, braced with vanity. They seem to trump common sense. But I passed muster.

The evening belonged to the musicians, and the music-lovers in attendance. Sir Charles Mackerras was a winner, and conducted the English Chamber Orchestra, along with Renée Fleming, another winner, in an extract from Porgy and Bess. The whole evening left everyone with a warm glow, and I was so pleased to have been able to do it.

I was anxious when Sheena agreed to present the Gramophone Awards at the Royal Festival Hall, in front of a live audience of more than 2,000. It's a high-end, glitzy occasion with the biggest names in classical music assembled under one roof. If she lost her way, or mangled her words, or exhibited the kind of confusion that I knew she was still experiencing, she would do so in front of a very high-powered audience.

I sat in the front row with an old friend from the BBC. My whole body was tensed with anticipation. I was actually afraid. But those senti-ments were also mixed with immense pride – pride at her courage and determination, but also at the esteem and affection that I felt sweep the auditorium the moment she came on to the stage. Two thousand people, every one of whom knew her story and knew that this was her first public appearance, cheered her to the echo, a prolonged ovation that washed

Figure 6.1 Sheena at the Gramophone Awards ceremony, 1999
Source: Alamy

over me in great echoing waves. My eyes stung. The clamour only ended when Sheena made a "calm down now" gesture with both hands and said the evening would be dedicated to celebrating great artists and that she would just be what she called "the grouting". I had a lump in my throat for two solid hours, as Sheena rattled through the programme, the names of composers and musical compositions tripping off her tongue flawlessly in Italian, French and German as well as English. It was draining though – for me as well as her. It was so public, and I knew that at any moment fatigue could overcome her and she'd start to lose her way. "Dr. Greasepaint will see me through," she'd said, and he did. After it was over, the colleague I'd sat beside told me I'd been gripping the arm of the chair so tightly that he could see the whites of my knuckles. We didn't stay for the reception afterwards. We went home and, again, Sheena slept for most of the next three days.

The Crown Prosecution Service charged the driver who had struck me, PC Glenn Whiteley, with "driving without due care and attention".

The trial took place at Horseferry Road Magistrates' Court in the autumn of 1999. I did not attend – but Allan did, and met me afterwards looking incredulous. The case had been dismissed. Allan remembers it to this day:

"Filtering through traffic" is an interesting euphemism for driving on the wrong side of the road. The driver later said he was on his way to an "emergency" – a Friday-night pub-brawl in a pub in Holloway Road. There were no skid marks on the road, even though the driver had said he'd braked when he saw Sheena step off the pavement and make her way to the centre of the road through the stationary cars queuing at the traffic lights.

Later, I was told that the van also had a dodgy speedometer and under-inflated tyres, but that the magistrate had not held these facts to be relevant. News coverage of the case was mixed. Some papers reported that the policeman in the passenger seat, PC Cubbon, had told the court that I had been "weaving" my way across the road, as if under the influence of alcohol, even though the police already had plenty of eyewitness statements saying that I had had a single glass of wine after attending a scholarly lecture. *The Scotsman* newspaper was one of the worst offenders. Its report was headlined, in big print, "TV presenter 'had been drinking'", with the rebuttal – that I'd had only one glass – buried in the last paragraph of the report. Allan wrote to *The Scotsman* and it published his letter. "I am extremely sad," he wrote, "that a newspaper we both respect so much, that is published in our own beloved home city, has played so thoughtless and cruel a part."

My mother wrote to *The Daily Telegraph*, which responded by pointing out that the paper did cover the fact that the magistrate rejected the suggestion that I was under the influence of alcohol at the time of the injury. So it did – but not until the following day. It seemed to me to be adding insult to injury in a literal sense – a deliberate attempt by the police to shift blame for what had happened to me. My father wrote to Sir Paul Condon, whose representative merely acknowledged receipt of the letter.

Perhaps the comment I appreciated most came from the cartoonist for the *Edinburgh Evening News*, Frank Boyle, who drew an ass in a wig, sitting on the magistrates' bench, passing judgement on the case brought by the Criminal Prosecution Service. "Not guilty," she is braying, as a police-van speeds past in the distance, and a prosecutor and police-officer shake hands caked in mud in the foreground.

Over the months, I was asked by many people for interviews. I did a few, with the *Sunday Herald*, the *Daily Mail*, with *The Daily*

Figure 6.2 Frank Boyle cartoon from the *Edinburgh Evening News*, 2000

Source: Frank Boyle, the *Edinburgh Evening News*

Telegraph – and with Simon Hattenstone of *The Guardian*, because I admired his writing. He wrote a good piece, and went on to write a longer article about police driving in general, so struck was he by my experience. He told me that he had been checking facts with a force far north of the Met. He was not writing about me, but the police PR he was speaking to said, "This isn't about the Sheena McDonald case, is it?" Thus I learned that I had graduated from "newsgirl", to "case" . . .

Being a journalist carries responsibilities – to be accurate, to interrogate interviewees fairly but fearlessly, to be impartial but NOT to deploy false moral equivalence. It can also offer a passport that opens doors and crosses borders like no other: so in the course of my years as a radio and TV reporter and presenter, I had met a range of men and women, some of them famous and fortunate – which may explain why the British press was interested in this particular brain-injury survivor: I had built a reputation as interviewer trusted by both the public and people I was interviewing. This had allowed me, over some 20 years, not only to highlight the achievements of unknown people but also to question the great and the good – and sometimes the downright bad.

Figure 6.3 Sheena and Allan in 2000
Source: Eamonn McCabe, *The Guardian*

In its glory days in the 1980s and 1990s, Channel 4 ran an hour-long weekly international affairs programme called *The World This Week*, which I presented for six years, before it was axed. It was unique in that it took a very internationalist rather than Brito-centric view of world affairs.

So the weekly round-table discussions were always peopled by non-British commentators or actual "players", and there was often the chance to interview the good, the bad and the less-than-prepossessing. The late King Hussein of Jordan came into the ITN studio to be interviewed live on a Saturday night, and was charming – and nervous. Muammar Gaddafi agreed to be interviewed from his tent in Libya in the run-up to the Gulf War, and tried to speak in his native tongue. We were again live on air, so I had to intervene.

Figure 6.4 Sheena at work in 1995, before the injury
Source: Channel 4 TV

President Gaddafi – I'm sorry to interrupt, but I know you speak good English, and I know that what you have to say is important, and that most of our viewers will not understand if you speak Arabic. Could you please speak in English?

And he smiled, and he did.

South African racist Eugene Terreblanche flew in to put his point of view. Aside from working hard at encouraging him to address the reality of the world we all share, I had to remain polite, in the face of his extraordinary halitosis.

And I flew to South Africa to interview Nelson Mandela, when he was not yet President, but was leader of the African National Congress. He agreed to do the interview as long as we were prepared to talk with him at 7.30 in the morning, on Wednesday 16 September 1992. Black Wednesday, the day when John Major's Conservative government was forced to withdraw the pound sterling from the European Exchange Rate Mechanism was, for me, the day I met a great human being.

The good and less-than-good are often available to journalists, because they want to get their personal message across. BBC current affairs programmes had permitted me to question senior politicians robustly, and a Channel 4 interview series brought "visionaries" to the small screen, via my carefully planned midwifing.

Robert Redford slipped into a hotel-room in New York, and spoke candidly about his films, his environmental ambitions and his standards. Nicholas Serota defended the most opaque contemporary examples of art – but said the one Tate artwork he would love to own personally would be a Constable painting.

Richard Rogers outlined his vision of a city that really works, departing from Le Corbusier, and putting the motor-car in its place.

Heroes and villains agreed to be interviewed – from Cyril Ramaphosa to Benjamin Netanyahu, from linguist Noam Chomsky, who had furrowed my brow when I was studying linguistics, to Russian arch-nationalist Vladimir Zhirinovsky, who sketched his vision of Russia's potential imperial reach from Scandinavia to India on a map with a red felt-tip pen.

My foray into television, following a few years working for Radio Scotland and Radio Aberdeen (which was effectively an invaluable apprenticeship), was with BBC Scotland, presenting the inspiringly titled *The Afternoon Show*, a very early example of daytime TV. I then spent six years at Scottish Television, where as a television interviewer I came face to face with many familiar names – Danny La Rue, not in drag at the time, and therefore very nervous; Rod Hull and Emu, demonstrating how much a man can imagine he will get away with when his hand and arm are encased in a sock; and poor old Hercules the Bear, who escaped his handler at the start of the live TV news show and prowled the studio ad lib as we tried to continue.

We pioneered big participation shows which brought together a representative cross-section of people in Scotland to discuss, sometimes with a senior politician present, issues of the day: one such was *Scottish Women* – and to this day I meet people who were invited to take part, and remember the experience fondly. Later, when at Channel 4, I did such shows with 300 participants.

My first ever TV interviewee, when a film student, was the late Quentin Crisp, scrupulously polite and charming, and unwilling to say a word which he hadn't previously written and published, in post-Wildean aphoristic style. Finally, I asked him, "Do you never say anything you haven't already constructed?" He looked shocked. "Oh no," he replied. "That would be frightfully careless."

But that was all before the injury. Now my efforts were more modest. I went back to Edinburgh for the first ever Scottish Politician of the Year Awards, given after dinner in the Royal Scottish Museum. I was one of five award-givers, and presented the top award of the night to the obvious choice – Donald Dewar, Scotland's first First Minister.

I was then invited to the annual global conference held by the broadcast news industry in Barcelona. I had taken part the previous year. "No," said Allan. "It's too far, you'll be too tired – and they want you to make an after-dinner speech. It's too much." But he was off to the United States for a week, so I said yes. I wanted to reflect the transition that news was going through, and the attempts by so many broadcasters to make it more entertaining. And then to say, "Do not patronise the viewer. Allow the viewer to understand what we do and why we do it, and treat him or her, and the news item, with respect."

Having a near-fatal setback had not modified my ambition. I knew that the top news professionals from around the world would be there, and was keen to demonstrate that I still existed, and could speak lucidly. I only had the energy to go for the closing dinner, and not the fascinating week-long conference. I sat beside a very brave cameraman, Sorious Samura, who I knew was about to win the Newsworld Personal Achievement award. He did not know that he had won this, but when presented with it spoke fluently and movingly about the need to report Sierra Leone, rather than the antics of disc-jockeys and popstars.

My own speech was very generously received:

> Far from never lying, the camera is the natural instrument of deception – whether it is to enhance, reduce, distance, contain or homogenize. To understand this no more undermines television's craft than decoding Santa destroys Christmas, or understanding the internal combustion engine reduces the pleasure of motoring. Not to understand it is to be ill-equipped to defend the best of its possible uses.

In preserving the mystery of the means by which broadcast material is achieved, programme-makers risk forfeiting the support of their staunchest potential allies, until now seen more as ratings-fodder than foot-soldiers in a battle for quality television. Unless the industry is willing to take viewers behind the mirrors, show them the false bottoms and trapdoors, the 57 varieties of oofle-dust that transform reality into news, then the misunderstanding, mistrust – above all, the alienation will continue. The best television in the world is an embattled and messy industry that needs the support of its immediate constituency, the viewers. We are being invited, as citizens, by all parties to enter the knowledge economy. Prime amongst our necessary skills should be to understand how information is mediated and how communications are controlled.

These words may read somewhat quaintly, but the world of social media and "citizen journalism" had yet to arrive.

Each of these efforts required managing my chronic fatigue. Every day, I was obliged to sleep in the afternoon for a few hours. "The best treatment for fatigue," Dr. Greenwood had said, "is exercise." I dutifully joined the local gym. What undermined any such activity was my uncontrolled appetite.

Fatigue

In December 1999, the main problem was fatigue. We implemented a diary system to monitor fatigue in relation to any work commitments or other activities. It is rare for individuals to accurately estimate what is possible when recovering from a TBI. It is different from running a marathon – you cannot push through and hope to recover quickly! I often explain that you need to work within your limit: every task takes greater effort and more energy. Why? Is this recovery or healing time? Perhaps yes, although I have never heard a full explanation of what is occurring. In lay terms, the brain is "mopping up" the debris and finding new or reinstating old connections.

One helpful analogy is the example of acute motor recovery following stroke. Nick Ward has demonstrated that in the first two weeks post-stroke, carrying out a simple motor movement recruits a large number of motor-related regions bilaterally in the left and right hemispheres of the brain.

After three months, the same movement recruits a smaller area of the motor-related brain regions (Ward *et al.*, 2004). The degree to which this process occurs was related to outcome; that is, the smaller the brain region required for the action, the better the outcome for that individual. In plain terms, this motor movement ideally becomes more efficient over time, recruiting a smaller brain region to do the job. It makes sense that this would also require less effort.

What causes fatigue and how can it be managed? Researchers have debated whether fatigue after TBI is the cause or result of sleepiness, anxiety and depression. Recent evidence, however, confirms the complexity of fatigue and that it is a cause, not a consequence, of these other factors (e.g., Bushnik *et al.*, 2015).

In practice, the concept of "interval training" is helpful. By this I mean undertaking an activity that is stimulating to the brain, followed by a specific period of time that involves no stimulation ("On-Off"). The bottom line is that recovering from a brain injury takes time!

The fatigue would last years. To begin with Sheena needed a good four hours solid sleep every afternoon. Again this, we were told, is typical for those in recovery from brain injury. I would use the time to read. There was no question of leaving Sheena to go out for a walk, in case she woke up disoriented. Gradually, as the months wore on, the need for sleep would diminish: the afternoon sleeps would shorten to three, then two hours. And, in time, there would be days when she didn't go to bed at all. On these days, sleep would come much earlier in the evening and last longer overnight. It was to be over three years before Sheena was able to do without daytime sleeping altogether.

Ten months after my injury, the world celebrated the 2,000th anniversary of the birth of Jesus Christ. The BBC marked this millennium with round-the-globe coverage, and sent Allan to Moscow, where he had been the correspondent. He said that I might accompany him.

As I remember, we spent a good week there. Boris Yeltsin stole the world's thunder and unexpectedly announced his retirement. This meant that Allan had some real news to report, unlike many millennial correspondents.

I remembered the previous Hogmanay enjoyed in Red Square, two months before the injury, dodging the rockets which Muscovites set off from their hands, and swigging Russian champagne, to the admiration of locals who were unaccustomed to seeing a Scotsman in his kilt bare his knees in the depths of winter. This year was different. Allan protectively suggested I watch the clock strike 12 from the vantage-point of a hotel window overlooking Red Square, so I did, in company with a couple of friends who had agreed to come with us to Moscow, and an unknown and very inebriated Scotsman. Allan himself was not there for midnight, so I found it somewhat anti-climactic. I began a new millennium by expressing my disappointment.

This was not a good idea. Allan saw my reaction as disproportionate, unrealistic and silly. Over a year later, he told me how the Moscow trip had really been. As was now customary, my self-perception had been over-rosy and far too positive. The reality, he told me, had been "a nightmare":

The BBC had asked me to go back to Moscow for a week. Thirty-first December 1999 was approaching and the newsroom wanted to have reporters stationed around the world as midnight broke. The Millennium would strike Moscow at 9 p.m. UK time.

I didn't want to leave Sheena on her own at New Year so asked her to come with me. I also persuaded another couple – again very old and trusted friends of Sheena's – to come too. We could all stay at my old flat in Moscow and although I would have to work on 31 December, we could have a few days there seeing the sights too. I knew I would need the help of the couple who came with us – that Sheena would be able to spend time with them while I was working.

On the afternoon of 31 December the Kremlin announced that Boris Yeltsin would step down as president of the Russian Federation at midnight, to be replaced as acting President by one Vladimir Putin, who was then Prime Minister. This was obviously big news, so of course I went to work.

Sheena blamed me, even though, theoretically, she had known that the reason we were there was that I was expected to work. She couldn't understand why I had "abandoned" her at midnight and was dismayed that she had had to toast the New Year "alone" (even though John and Sue were with her). More and more she saw me as choosing the BBC over her, resenting with a growing intensity everything in my life – my friends as well as my work – that wasn't principally about my life with her. Her horizons had shrunk. I didn't know whether they'd ever expand again. And, increasingly, she wanted me constantly inside those horizons too, and resented any part of my life that lay beyond them.

I knew this was unsustainable. But I didn't know what to do about it.
I was still in my 30s. How was I going to have the working life I wanted?
The answer, though it would take me another year to understand it and
accept it, was simple: I couldn't.

Allan: the transition from boyfriend to carer

It is often those closest to the person who sustained a TBI that suffer in silence. Allan had gone from being the boyfriend who lived overseas as a foreign correspondent to main carer overnight. It is true that many relationships do not survive this major change in roles. There are many studies documenting the negative impact of TBI on marital relationships, especially for severe TBI and as time goes on and the reality sets in after the first few years (for review see Ponsford et al., 1995). Inevitable are changes in roles, some temporary during the acute and post-acute hospitalisation period or during neurorehabilitation and community reintegration, and some changes are permanent. Partners as carers may be unwilling to communicate as fully as pre-TBI, or the content and nature of communication changes as it may be focused on rehabilitation strategies or practical aspects of care.

I am in awe of Allan's dedication and astute observations that played a key role in Sheena's recovery. However, I can recall moments when I realised that he was holding on by a thread. At these times, I saw my role as providing stability and support for both Sheena and Allan. It is important to create a safe space where couples can come and freely speak about what is occurring. It is important to reflect on and explain what is happening and why, in relation to the TBI and stage of recovery. Then it is possible to identify key actions that will potentially address or change the situation. This is done collaboratively; Allan typically knew what to do, but he needed understanding and reframing of the problem, and to be heard and supported. Developing trust between the three of us was key, so that Sheena and Allan allowed me into their personal lives and relationship and so I could enlist one or both in specific strategies.

I knew that I must restrain my doggy affection for Allan. One day, he announced that I was overloading him with expectation. He needed space. I realised that I had been expecting this response: my life had been so limited by the injury that I had consequently limited his life, not least due to my reliance on his company and care.

The first anniversary of the injury happened when Allan was work-ing abroad, and was my longest separation from him for a year. So I went to the theatre, alone. I had chosen to spend most of my adult life alone, but now wanted company. If Allan still preferred to live alone, albeit with the companionship of his daily workmates, then so be it. But life suddenly seemed very short. I could not remember why I had ever thought living alone was preferable to being with someone else. I now predicted that one day Allan would wake up and think, "This is not me! I'm a lone wolf, forever pirouetting the globe to report on disasters and wars." Should I exploit the Leap Year tradition and propose, I won-dered? Probably not.

The overeating; the weight gain; the lack of knowledge of either; the impulse buying; the slightly disinhibited social behaviour; the "tangen-tial talking": I thought of all of these as functions of the same thing – a basic lack of self-awareness, an inability to monitor one's own conduct and behaviour.

This posed a very acute problem for me. I was exhausted by the constant effort of gently trying to steer Sheena away from these behav-iours, or to try to disguise them from others, even family and close friends, because I wanted people to believe that Sheena was making "a full recovery". But I wanted her to participate in her own recovery. The question was: how to make her aware of what she was doing, on all these fronts, without being confrontational? Without dispiriting and demoralising her?

This is the role that Gail Robinson played in our lives over more than five years. The only place where I could raise these matters in a non-confrontational way was in Gail's consulting room at Queen Square. There I could talk about the things that I was struggling with directly to Gail, rather than with Sheena, but with Sheena present, listening to me describing my experience of her recovery. I worked hard at express-ing myself in ways that didn't sound as though I was blaming Sheena or challenging her. And I think, subliminally, I was saying that I now needed her to help me to help her continue.

Frontal "executive" functions: self-awareness and social judgement

In the first two years post-TBI, I met with Sheena and Allan together and separately. One of the main themes that emerged, with insightful observations from Allan, was that Sheena's monitoring mechanism could be problematic. This took the form of failing to monitor on several levels: the topic of conversation and whether her contribution in terms of quality and quantity of content was appropriate; disinhibition of both speech and behaviours (as previously discussed excess eating and buying); and, as in the example of the plumber, judgement as to who to share what with! *Anosognosia* or a lack of awareness of difficulties is common after TBI, especially when the right hemisphere of the brain is damaged and when changes or difficulties are subtle. This can be extremely difficult to change, but it is possible to increase self-awareness of subtle difficulties with clear and immediate feedback.

First, in hindsight most of these difficulties were predictable from Sheena's "inefficient" performance on the Hayling Sentence Completion Test in her neuropsychological reassessment in August 1999. This test has become a favourite of mine as it assesses verbal initiation, inhibition and use of a strategy, all with the same task. Subtle verbal disinhibition is associated with damage to the right inferior frontal lobe (see Robinson et al., 2015) and, with my students, I have recently shown that this also occurs in healthy ageing (Gibson et al., 2018). Sheena's follow-up brain MRI in 2003 revealed areas of focal damage that included the right inferior frontal lobe, as well as left posterior temporal and occipital regions.

Second, how do we target social judgement and appropriateness in a way that maintains dignity and confidence yet tackles the core problem? The key to this was Allan and his relationship with Sheena. The three of us together would discuss situations in our sessions and I would probe details and gently ask what might be appropriate. I obtained agreement from Sheena that we would enlist Allan to provide timely and immediate feedback when these situations occurred, with the aim of increasing awareness. There was a clear point about two years post-TBI when Allan requested a session alone that signalled to Sheena that things must change and she would need to fully participate in this. Allan had reached his capacity for coping alone. I recognised that addressing this issue and enlisting both as a team were crucial at this key turning point for both Sheena's recovery and their relationship.

My return to work remained gradual. It owed much to a curious cocktail of popular ignorance and short-term celebrity. I was grateful to those courageous souls who harboured no prejudice – or perhaps no knowledge – about what a brain-injury might and often can do, and to those who thought that the best help that they could offer me was a little work. What I did have to do was monitor my responses to offers of work with care. When you are trying to recover from a brain-injury, do not force yourself to work harder than your capacity allows: you will fail. A brain-injury changes what is possible. No matter how regularly you have burned the candle at both ends before the injury, you cannot revive such behaviour.

A year after the injury, Allan and I were both in London. Allan was working hard on the two-hour BBC documentary about the previous year's events in Kosovo. And I was presenting BBC Radio 4's *The Week in Westminster*. It felt good to talk about things other than brain injury and police driving. I found I had to work very hard to call on my previous skills at absorbing information, and using it to inform incisive, relevant questioning. Amongst my guests was the wife of a surgeon; she cheerfully told me that her husband had read about me and said that I definitely would not recover. I still had to spend an hour or two sleeping in the afternoon, but I got away with it, I thought. Gail told me to go easy, and not to take on too much.

I was asked by ITV to report and present a documentary for Channel 4 called *Deadly Pursuit*, about police driving (but not about my case). The producer/director Ninder Billing was checking facts with a police representative who finally responded to her questions: "You make me think of this woman I've heard about who's making a programme accusing the police of driving too fast or out of control." There was a pause. Ninder said, "I am working with that woman."

What we found out was interesting. For instance, there was no statutory national standard for the training of police drivers. Each police force in the country operates within the ethos of "operational independence", which is operative when it is considered directly appropriate; some activities must meet national minimum standards – but not police driving. The Association of Chief Police Officers now invites every force to follow a set of guidelines – but guidelines are not requirements.

I was tired after filming around the country for *Dispatches*, and had missed my afternoon nap for two long days. I mused – was this as good as life would get? I imagined how life post-injury might have been – unable to concentrate or perform the merest cognitive task. I should be thankful, I thought. But I was tempted to mourn what I had lost – independence, energy, full sight. Yield not to temptation! – I upbraided myself. Half Scots, half Yorkshire, I determined not to lapse into self-pity.

Allan was now working full time again.

I was grappling with decisions about my own professional future. I'd been a career foreign correspondent. During the early months of Sheena's convalescence, I had gone back to work gradually. The BBC had asked me to present the Today *programme on Radio 4, which was a huge privilege and, for me, an immense challenge. It meant a 3 a.m. alarm call, into work by 4 a.m., on the air at 6 a.m., and off again at 9 a.m. I could be home by 9.30 and spend most of the day there. It was ideal, but it was never going to be my longterm future.*

My Kosovo project ended in March. The BBC asked me whether I'd like to take up my old post as Southern Africa Correspondent in Johannesburg – a post I'd left in 1997. I said yes. I knew the patch, loved South Africa and had many friends there. Sheena would move there with me. You can live well in Johannesburg, I told myself; we'd stay there a couple of years until Sheena was much better and then reassess.

This would prove to be a daft and, again, hopelessly unrealistic decision. When I look back on it now I see how, even now, I had still not fully understood what had happened to us.

References

Bushnik, T., Caplan, B., Bogner, J., Brenner, L., Ponsford, J., Schönberger, M. and Rajaratnam, S.M. (2015). "A model of fatigue following traumatic brain injury". *Journal of Head Trauma Rehabilitation*, 30(4), 277–282.

Gibson, E.C., Barker, M.S., Martin, A.K. and Robinson, G.A. (2018). "Initiation, inhibition and strategy generation across the healthy adult lifespan". *Archives of Clinical Neuropsychology*. https://doi.org/10.1093/arclin/acy057

Ponsford, J., Sloan, S. and Snow, P. (1995). *Traumatic Brain Injury: Rehabilitation for Everyday Adaptive Living*. Hove: Lawrence Erlbaum Associates.

Ritchie, L., Wright-St Clair, V.A., Keogh, J. and Gray, M. (2014). "Community integration after traumatic brain injury: a systematic review of the clinical implications of measurement and service provision for older adults". *Archives of Physical Medicine and Rehabilitation*, 95, 163–174.

Robinson, G.A., Cipolotti, L., Walker, D.G., Biggs, V., Bozzali, M. and Shallice, T. (2015). "Verbal suppression and strategy use: a role for the right lateral prefrontal cortex?". *Brain*, 138(4), 1084–1096.

Ward, N.S., Brown, M.M., Thompson, A.J. and Frackowiak, R.S. (2004). "The influence of time after stroke on brain activations during a motor task". *Annals of Neurology*, 55(6), 829–834.

Chapter 7

Life after near-death

Allan had agreed to take up the post of Southern Africa correspondent in April 2000 and asked me to join him. I said yes. Although I knew no-one there, my relationship with him seemed more important than anything. He did not want to marry, though, which left me with a streak of insecurity. He said that marriage only made sense if you had children. But he had been so caring and generous. I credited him to a great extent for my apparently unexpected recovery. He had encouraged me to use my battered body and brain. Experiencing a very severe brain-injury, which had left me with reduced eyesight and possibly lifelong fatigue, seemed bearable.

But I would have to see through the civil case against the Metropolitan Police before any thought of flying to the southern hemisphere.

I was kidding myself. For a start you can't live well in Johannesburg unless you can drive. Sheena wouldn't want to do that, even though she had passed the eyesight test. I had also underplayed in my mind the amount of travel the job had involved. In my previous stint in Southern Africa I had spent weeks at a time working away from my home base – in Zaire, Rwanda, Sierra Leone and elsewhere. The obvious question was what Sheena could do, alone in Johannesburg, when I was on these extended work trips, and I pushed this question to the back of my mind.

I was, I would see later, still trying to reassemble life as it had been before the injury, still unable to accept that it had changed completely the trajectory of our lives.

My designated lawyer in the civil case, Keith Taylor at Thomsons, warned me that the case would take time – a long time. I would wait, I said, as long as need be. I was now curious about how justice is implemented in the United Kingdom. I had received many letters and heard tales from citizens who felt that they had been treated unjustly. A family friend who is a Law Lord had told me that the law is indeed haphazard, unreliable and whimsical. Keith Taylor went on to warn me that I was a "profile case", which the Met might feel they could not afford to lose. I wondered what this meant in practice.

As part of the preparation for the civil suit, Keith Taylor arranged for me to be examined by an independent psychologist in Harley Street, Dr. Nicholas Leng. After an hour answering his questions, he shook his head. "This is remarkable," he said. "Ninety per cent of people who suffered the injuries you experienced would not have recovered. Your case is exceptional. I can't tell you why – we don't know that much about how the brain can repair itself. All I can tell you is that you have been unbelievably lucky – it may have something to do with your brain-capacity or discipline, but we really don't know."

He went on to tell me that fatigue could well be a lifelong problem, and that my eyesight would probably be permanently damaged.

Both these things I had been told before, but I heard his words with a new sense of chill. I might have been "unbelievably lucky", but I had also been very unlucky.

Dr. Leng's written report later concluded that I had "superior intellectual ability and a rewarding job prior to the 'accident'."

He further referred me to an independent psychiatrist at the Maudsley Hospital in south London. This was to prove catalytic.

We were now seeing Gail Robinson on a regular basis. Splitting my time between Edinburgh and London allowed me to keep regular appointments with her every five or six weeks, usually accompanied by Allan. These meetings proved to be invaluable: 40 minutes describing my new world and hearing her counsel served to furnish me with a steady framework for my now unpredictable days and weeks – although my discipline was poor. Gail repeatedly recommended that I now keep a food diary, in order to monitor my excessive eating. I repeatedly failed.

In May 2000, the National Hospital in Queen Square launched an Acute Brain Injury Service, the first of its kind in London. I was invited to say a few words. "This unit is the clinical equivalent of joined-up government." Allan was there, sitting beside a doctor who had no idea that Allan knew me. "That woman," said the doctor, "is a miracle."

Acute Brain Injury Unit (ABIU)

The Acute Brain Injury Unit (ABIU) at the National Hospital started in February 2000. It was a unique service that accepted patients in the acute stage following both TBI and stroke. The key was coordinated care and the integration of acute medical treatments alongside neurorehabilitation by a specialist multidisciplinary team (Consultant neurology, TBI and Stroke nurse specialists, physiotherapy, occupational therapy, speech and language therapy, dietician, clinical neuropsychology). Most patients stayed between two and eight weeks, with the average stay about three weeks, and then they were discharged either to home or to post-acute neurorehabilitation units.

I was very involved at the start of the ABIU when we developed policies and procedures and it became a model of care that was held up as a beacon of hope in the NHS. In fact, the ABIU team won a Nuffield Travel Fellowship and, in 2002, eight of us travelled to Melbourne, Australia, to visit a number of stroke units and learn about governance procedures. Later, in 2006, with Barbara Wilson and the Oliver Zangwill Centre team, as an ABIU representative I was invited to St Petersburg, Russia, to discuss models of neurorehabilitation that could be adapted to fit their health care system. At this time, I received several invitations to talk about neuropsychological rehabilitation and particularly the model developed for the ABIU (and BINJ clinic). The ABIU remains unique in combining TBI and stroke, and in the integration of medical treatment alongside allied health care and multidisciplinary neurorehabilitation.

Dr. Richard Greenwood was the lead clinician for the ABIU. As Sheena's consultant, he brought many of the principles of care to both her acute management when she was still in post-traumatic amnesia on the John Young ward, and then later through the BINJ Clinic, which precipitated her outpatient neuropsychological rehabilitation with me. I am of the view that it was Richard's vast experience with brain injury that was foundational to the development of both the ABIU and BINJ Clinic services at the National Hospital, and to the excellent care individuals like Sheena have received for more than 20 years now.

Dividing my time between London and Edinburgh led to a double life in more ways than one: that of an (occasional) broadcast journalist and at the same time that of a trauma-survivor in long-term recovery. The most obvious indicator of the latter life was my continuing weight-gain. And the post-traumatic behaviour continued: talking and laughing immoderately, and now crying uncontrollably too.

The following month, I was assessed at the Maudsley Hospital by Professor Declan Murphy. Over the course of two hours, he asked questions that no-one else had asked: what was I going to do now? What were my plans? How was I going to make a living? How did I feel about what had happened? Did I think about the "accident"? Did I bottle things up?

I broke down and could not speak. I snuffled for a good ten minutes. At the end of the session and the best part of a box of tissues, Professor Murphy declared that I was clinically depressed, and recommended antidepressant medication coupled with cognitive behavioural therapy.

"I don't want to be depressed," I wailed.

"I don't want to be short," said the professor. He is.

When I told Gail about the session at our next meeting, I broke down again and could not speak for some minutes.

"Well, that's progress," said Gail. I had been warned when at the Astley Ainslie that I might experience depression at some point. In retrospect, in the early months of recovery I was most probably suffering from the consequences of an extreme blow to my frontal lobes: I had lost the ability to react, whether it be to feel happy or angry or sad – a condition called anosognosia. This is a state, as I understand it, in which one's self-awareness is adversely affected, to the extent that one can suffer very dark days with an apparent smile, Pollyanna-like.

It was not only psychologists who foresaw depression. A dear friend who had undergone a mastectomy some years before told me how depression crept up on her six months after the operation: "I just grit my teeth, and put my head down and got on with it." At the time, I thanked my stars that this had never happened to me. Now it had.

Gail said that my depression was a positive sign that I was at last tuning in to genuine emotions, and a very reasonable grief over what I had lost, in terms of time, and what I now lived with – the physical and mental consequences of the injury. She encouraged me to plan long-term, to think seriously about what I wanted to do, to express myself honestly and not to pretend that all was well when it was not, nor to feel guilty about my true feelings. Allan was with me and was supportive.

So my depression suggested that I was finally facing up to the enormity of what had happened, complemented by realising my personal insignificance.

There had been hints of this in the preceding months. In November 1999, when my eye test had diagnosed long-term damage to the occipital lobe, I had gone home mournful. Allan had been in Kosovo, so there had been no immediate comfort. And I had been rattled by a recent conversation over lunch with (erstwhile) Channel 4 colleagues, who had revealed that I would not be presenting Channel 4 News again. I politely accepted this, but went home dejected.

Sheena had never had to hustle for work. It came to her. She was in demand. At a time when our trade – broadcast journalism – was still overwhelmingly male, she'd made a stellar reputation as a broadcaster of unusually high intelligence. She had a beautiful television presence, but it was her intellect that distinguished her.

In the early days of her tentative recovery – just a few days after the injury – I'd gone to see Sheena's London GP. She asked me to visit her at home and have dinner with her and her husband. "Let's face it," she said casually over pre-dinner drinks, "I don't think we're going to see Sheena on TV again are we love?" I felt I'd had a bucket of icy water emptied over me. I made up my mind that I didn't want to see this woman again. I got through dinner as quickly as courtesy allowed and left, determined not to accept what she'd said.

But the question of work was something we'd have to deal with. Channel 4 didn't waste much time in dropping Sheena from its schedules and its plans. Her contract with them was coming to an end anyway. But I felt let down by the company to whom she'd given what would turn out to be the best years of her working life.

It took me over a week – and a fairly tearful week – to begin to come to terms with this. I thought that they had made a mistake. Anosognosia meant that my confidence in my own ability remained unshaken, but my hopes of being accepted as a walking, talking survivor were severely dented; and I knew that I would be financially challenged. Allan tried to be supportive: "They've had their chance. Forget them. The BBC has been really generous to you, unlike Channel 4. I wish now that you'd done your programme about police driving for *Panorama*." The BBC had been good to me. I was still doing interview and discussion-programmes for the World Service and Radio 4, and maintaining contact with BBC Two. And in truth, Channel 4 had given me work and pay for years before the injury.

I simply was now not aware that, at least for the moment, live broadcasting was beyond me.

Work, depression and sense of self: reality hits

In 2000, I regularly met with Sheena as Allan was working in South Africa. It was in June of this year that Sheena came face-to-face with reality. At some point, it was inevitable that awareness and insight would increase alongside returning to work. For Sheena, experience living with the consequences of TBI in terms of fatigue, subtle executive difficulties and the weight gain had accumulated. Added to that were the frank questions and feedback from this new set of experts for her civil case. The final straw was that her previous employers closed a door. Until you realise exactly what the TBI means for your daily life in real terms, understanding the loss and what has changed can only remain an abstract concept. Being directly confronted with questions about the future and having a previous major work role on television cease precipitated a new level of awareness in Sheena. With this came a wave of grief and a period of depression. In Sheena's case, this happened about 15 months post-TBI, which is typical for the onset of depression. As Sheena reflected, this was not possible when the frontal lobes are still unable to reflect or provide a level of self-awareness that integrates information from many sources, including emotional responses. In the frontal lobe function framework detailed in an earlier chapter, both the *behavioural and emotional self-regulation* and *metacognitive* functions are required. In general, depression following a TBI emerges late (i.e. > one year) once you can appreciate changes (Fleminger, 2008; Rapoport, 2012). Kreutzer and colleagues (2001), for example, found that about 40% of TBI patients presented with major depressive symptoms about two-and-a-half years post-TBI. The triggers for this vary depending on individual and contextual factors.

Often, cognitive behavioural therapy can be effective in addressing mood symptoms, including depression. The psychiatrist Declan Murphy recommended anti-depressants in combination with cognitive behaviour therapy. I worked with a colleague that provided this for individuals like Sheena; however, this did not appeal to her. So we continued with our sessions and incorporated an approach to target and improve mood. We focused on increasing

Figure 7.1 Sheena and Gail at the National Hospital
Source: Suki Dhanda, *The Observer*

and noting pleasant activities and we monitored and challenged automatic negative thoughts. At the same time Sheena also started a serotonin-based medication. This immediately provided a buffer from her "gloominess". I am also of the view it is best to go through grief and feel the loss, rather than avoidance. My experience is that it rarely dissipates when ignored!

Over the next few months a routine of exercise with a few regular work engagements became the foundation of moving through the grief cycles. By October, Sheena was proactively choosing work depending on her level of interest and fatigue. A new goal emerged to write and journal about her experience. This was a useful exercise in developing discipline and training concentration. Sheena also started to develop a new awareness of herself and noticed changes such as a decrease in her sense of smell and not noticing temperature changes.

A new topic emerged regarding memory. After the TBI retrograde amnesia was present as Sheena had lost access to some of her old memories. This quickly resolved and was minimal. However, almost two years post-TBI,

Sheena became aware that her old autobiographical (or episodic) memories seemed a little vague in some ways. This contrasted with good clear knowledge of semantic memories for public events. This theme ran through the next few years and Sheena was extremely curious about how one could have a sense of self without these memories. The documentary that Sheena made, *Who Am I Now?*, explored the nature of consciousness and identity when the "self" is disrupted and memories lost.

It was more than a year later when Sheena started to come to terms with the seriousness of her TBI. In September 2001, I noted that Sheena had wondered if this was as good as it gets, and that she may never be the same. Yes, this is the point when I know that a major shift has occurred. Sheena had finally understood that things had changed, but at the same time, life was full of opportunities. Soon after this, with Allan, we talked about her vision for the future.

There are clear dangers in going back to work too soon. If you don't meet the professional standards you achieved before the injury, your colleagues and potential employers will be unforgiving. Sheena had succeeded at the Gramophone Awards and in the Foreign Ministers panel at the Commonwealth Summit in Durban. But it didn't always go well. Before the injury she'd presented a daily politics programme at lunchtime on Channel 4. In early 2000, more than a year after the injury, they asked her back to present a special edition to discuss the forthcoming London mayoral election. Ken Livingstone, who was the favourite to win, was one of the live guests. I watched at home. I was full of apprehension. Sheena looked and sounded fine to begin with but I could tell she was beginning to become weary and at one point she appeared to forget that she was presenting the programme and that it was up to her to steer the whole thing. There was a pause after someone spoke and Sheena smiled at what had been said and seemed to be waiting for something else to happen. I was mortified. Television magnifies everything. Ken Livingstone then intervened by making another point and it seemed to me that he had seen what had happened and decided to rescue the situation – and rescue Sheena. I was heartbroken. She had not gotten away with it this time. I don't think she even knew what had happened: her ability to monitor her own behaviour was improving, but it still wasn't back to anywhere near her pre-injury level of functioning. I decided to say nothing.

Within two weeks of starting to take the serotonin-based drug Cipramil, I began to perk up. Things felt less bleak. I had work – less than previously, but almost enough to keep body and soul together, and I had friends. Why was I complaining? I took the advice to book a session of cognitive behavioural therapy at a clinic in Wimpole Street, but found it underwhelming – and expensive. One session was one too many, I decided. I would stick to drugs.

One hard truth faced by a survivor of any trauma is the immediate effect on one's income and finances. My "survivor-celebrity" status had run its term. The phone had gone quiet. There is a natural cut-off point to public sympathy and interest. I might now be making an extraordinary and textbook-defying recovery but I had to face the bleak truth that the road ahead would be stony. I would have to initiate new work for myself.

I was servicing two mortgages, one in London and one in Edinburgh, and now earning practically nothing. My savings were dwindling fast – and no friends or relations had funds to spare for my welfare. I was saved from penury thanks to Alexander Querns, a financial adviser who, almost 20 years previously, had recommended to me a critical injury insurance policy. The monthly premiums had been predictably steep, but when I went freelance in my 20s, he had persuaded me that they were a wise investment since no employer existed to give me sick pay should it ever be needed. He now took me out for lunch. "I think your case qualifies for the redemption of this policy," he said – and it did. The £100,000 I received served to keep the wolf from the door for some years.

Allan, meanwhile, analysed my mortgage costs, and figured out that they could be enormously reduced.

I was still suffering chronic fatigue, and beginning to realise that this was a long game. And I was at last coming to acknowledge the unpleasant new reality that having been severely underweight, I was now seriously overweight.

One day in a taxi in London Sheena gestured toward a young woman in the street. She was very overweight. It was a hot day and she was wearing an ill-fitting t-shirt and struggling to pull a backpack onto her shoulders. The effort was making her red in the face. "Am I as big as her?" Sheena said. "Yes," I said. "Nearly." She was shocked. Clearly she had had no idea. When she looked at herself in the mirror she simply saw herself, and failed to register all the weight that had piled on.

"Just eat less," said Allan. He was right, but my attempts fell foul of my now characteristic tendency to confabulate. Oh yes, I would tell myself and everyone else, I've cut right down. But the scales told a different story. Vanity can take a long time to kick in after a brain-injury. Gail's efforts to engender dietary self-discipline in me were unsuccessful. I remained amazed by Allan's dedication and patience in relation to me. He was always, work allowing, only a phone-call away, and throughout the first year of my recovery, had been a constant presence. He monitored and moderated my behaviour, and helped me negotiate this brave new world I now inhabited. In fact, as my principal carer, he now had a second fulltime job.

Whenever Sheena vented her frustration on me, I tried, always, to remember that it was the injury speaking. There were moments of determined negativity, when nothing I did or said was good enough; everything had to interpreted in the most negative light. There was an increasing resort to passive-aggressive defence: "Oh of course you must be right because I've had a brain injury, why should anybody, least of all you, listen to anything I say?"

There is no way to answer that doesn't lend itself to more negative interpretation. I tried, and didn't always succeed, to avoid escalating, to avoid biting back. One day, at home, after Sheena had said something barbed and unkind and unanswerable, I said, without planning it,

I've got nothing left. I'm emptied out. There's nothing left in me to offer to make this better. I'm going out for a walk. I'll be back in 20 minutes and when I come back, it's your turn. It's your turn to think of something to make this better. Your turn to think about how I'm feeling in all of this.

It felt selfish. But I had felt utterly defeated. And when I came back Sheena was quiet and simply hugged me without saying anything and we stayed like that, in silence, for a long while.

I think gradually we understood that this was a shared enterprise; that we had to understand, to work out, how Sheena could play a role in her own recovery and in mine, for my life had been derailed by that police van that night and I too was a survivor in recovery; we had to understand what we could do to progress our shared recovery as a partnership, as a couple – and how, crucially, she could help me through this as much as I was trying to help her.

In June it was time to move to Johannesburg. Sheena was getting more offers of work. These meant a lot to her and I saw that the work that was coming in was contributing to her recovery. She decided not to come to Johannesburg: she would, instead, come often to visit, as she had done during my previous foreign postings. I went to Johannesburg and tried to throw myself into the job the way I had done the first time I'd taken up the post, six years earlier.

Within a few weeks I had accepted it wouldn't work. It was impossible to be apart from Sheena. Our lives had wrapped themselves around each other so fully that we had to be together.

On my next trip to London I went to see my boss. "It has been a mistake to go back," I said to him. "I thought it would be like it was the first time I was there. But everything's different now. I don't think I can stay." He was a thoughtful and decent man. "I have to ask you to do it for a year," he said. "And during that year we'll think about what to do with you next."

I'd already done three months. I would now be counting the days, even as I rushed to the airport to take a flight to Congo or Nairobi or Freetown.

That, for me, was, I think, the end of the journey that began on that grim winter's day in Moscow when I had taken the phone call in my flat and heard the news that Sheena had been run over. It had taken 18 months to understand that there would be no going back to normal. The normal we'd known had ended with a police van driving on the wrong side of the road at midnight on a north London street. Finally I had come to understand it, and accept it.

When he began to spend more time abroad again, our relationship sometimes suffered. I felt that he tended to over-compensate for his absence when he returned, reminding me of my ongoing frailties, and warning me to control my newfound self. I attempted to bite my tongue with good grace, for I guess his assessment of me was probably more or less accurate, and because I knew that he had suffered. "Secondary trauma" is the term used to describe what relatives of injured people experience.

Others close to me coped in their own ways with what had happened. My mother abruptly took to her bed, and slept for days on end. Her GP was mystified, and all her various anti-depressant prescriptions failed to hit the mark. After a couple of months of self-imposed sleep therapy, Ma came round.

My father, a retired Church of Scotland minister, prayed – as many people told me they did, including the man who calls himself a "Presbyterian agnostic" – Allan. My sister abandoned her lifelong "little sister" persona, while my sister-in-law became the family peacemaker. Many friends rallied round.

I thought more than before about the point of it all. I decided that there are many reasons to live. We all can give, and are all valuable. Some of us have children, some are artists, some bus drivers, some surgeons. Some are kind to neighbours, some smile at strangers.

After taking Cipramil for over a year, I elected to stop. I never felt the need to return to it. But two years on from the injury I was still tired, with no energy reserves. I could now, if work demanded it, get through a whole day, but needed to make up the lost sleep on subsequent days. People again said, "Oh, I feel like that – it's age!" and I smiled. Mine was not the fatigue that comes with age but a condition far more immediate and demanding and irresistible.

I resolved to visit Allan in South Africa for the second post-injury Christmas. I arrived on Christmas Day after doing a presenting job for BBC Radio 4 in Paris on 23 December.

Allan met me at the airport and took me to his new home, decorated and festive. We had a lovely day, followed by a couple of days on safari. Then he was unexpectedly scrambled to Zimbabwe, so I had to head home earlier than planned. On our last night together, Allan invited a friend round so was late to bed – where he instantly embarked on what he later called "a wobbly". He accused me of using him, of abusing his good nature and tolerance, of dismissing his friends – all in all, a classic tiff.

Thinking about things, flying home, I realised that this was the inevitable consequence of his being thrown into the role of carer, and getting nothing back except increasing dependency. I must stand on my own two feet, I resolved. But the uneasy joust continued for some months, off and on. Perhaps, I wondered, it was a side-effect of living so far apart. His life, rightly, was where he lived – Africa – but he disliked hearing me say that because it prompted him to feel guilty. I read that 75% of relationships do not survive injuries like mine, whether or not the partners are married.

So when Allan elected after a year in South Africa to come back, I had modest expectations.

References

Fleminger, S. (2008). "Long-term psychiatric disorders after traumatic brain injury". *European Journal of Anaesthesiology*, 25(S42), 123–130.

Kreutzer, J.S., Seel, R.T. and Gourley, E. (2001). "The prevalence and symptom rates of depression after traumatic brain injury: a comprehensive examination". *Brain Injury*, 15(7), 563–576.

Rapoport, M.J. (2012). "Depression following traumatic brain injury". *CNS Drugs*, 26(2), 111–121.

Chapter 8

Plodding on

I was hired to report on and present a BBC World Service series on domestic violence, gathering material and reporting from Nicaragua, where there was a pioneering programme aimed at rehabilitating and reforming abusive men. I actively enjoyed this – and the financial fillip.

Aside from trying to re-fashion a portfolio of work, I was preparing for the civil case against the Met, the Crown Prosecution Service (CPS) action against the police driver having been dismissed. I had been grievously injured, thereby potentially obliging someone to care for me or to pay for my care. I could not count on Allan forever. I was no longer driving despite being permitted to do so. I had lost actual and potential earnings.

I wanted justice to be done. It goes without saying that I had not received an apology or an admission of culpability from anyone. I remembered an incident I had been involved in, some years before, in Edinburgh city centre. A car whizzed down the road, through a red light and slap-bang into the side of my car. I was seriously shaken – so much so that when the driver of the other car jumped out and started haranguing me for causing the injury myself, I wondered if he was right. Eyewitnesses approached and confirmed that he was entirely in the wrong, and his insurance company eventually covered all costs. It turned out he actually worked for the insurance company. This was clearly a familiar tactic – to try immediately to shift the blame for any event onto the other person involved. Parting lovers often try the same trick.

I could not now look at a policeman. I turned away whenever a police vehicle drove by. I knew that forgiveness was necessary, and I kept failing to find ways of reaching that peaceful place.

"Compensation" has become something of a dirty word in Britain these days, as lawyers climb onto the US bandwagon and advertise their services as agents for anyone seeking financial redress for any wrong done to them.

I did not consider my legal action to be at all grasping. Rather, it strikes me as regrettable that the perpetrators of egregious misdeeds, such as the one from which I suffered, had to be forced to admit their folly. We are encouraged to admire the police. Hardly a night passes without the television schedules including some dramatic fictional depiction of police life. I remember when *Z-Cars* started in the 1960s, which at the time was a bold modernisation of the Dixon of Dock Green image. It moved from the bobby on the beat to the copper in the car, whizzing around to apprehend criminals. Now, from *Prime Suspect* to *Line of Duty* to *Spiral*, a police drama is a ratings winner.

Is this really what Sir Robert Peel envisaged when he brought about the Metropolitan Police Act in 1829, and gave rise to the homonymous "bobbies" on the beat? Ironically, he died from injuries following a road traffic injury (RTI), involving the popular mode of transport at the time – he was thrown off a horse in 1850.

So the police in Britain have not been part of our society for long, but we now depend on them to "keep the peace". If we are burgled, we call the police. If we are attacked or raped, we call the police. If we are worried about crowd control or traffic, we expect the police to manage things. Political parties vie to assure the electorate that there will be more police than ever before under their governance.

What is never pledged or even suggested is an effective accountability mechanism. Who sanctions them to do as they do? Who monitors their actions? Who trusts them?

Police spokesmen repeatedly claim to be improving their training procedures. Back in 1998, the House of Commons was told that the Association of Chief Police Officers (ACPO) had provided forces with detailed guidelines on police driver training. "Such training is progressive," MPs were told.

> However, it is ultimately for individual chief constables to determine the extent of training received by their officers and how they are deployed . . . The key issue is the need to train officers so they are capable of understanding modern road conditions and exercise all due care when travelling at speeds and in conditions beyond those experienced by the general motorist.
>
> Hansard Written Answers for 22 April 1998

In December 2000, ACPO launched a national training guide setting out minimum standards for police drivers. At the launch, the Chief Constable of Sussex Police called it "a positive step forward", and the

Driving Standards Agency representative said it would lead to "a reduction in the number of accidents and incidents in which police vehicles are involved." Has it?

Ultimately, the police forces are accountable to the Home Secretary. Indirectly, that means that they are accountable to you and I, but in practice this is a dysfunctional relationship. There is a small and under-funded body called the Police Complaints Authority which tries to investigate matters referred to it, but the onus is on the citizen to lodge a complaint and the entire process is, by definition, post hoc. In December 2000, the Government announced the establishment of a new body – an independent police complaints commission. This came six months after Liberty, the human rights organisation, published a report recommending the establishment of such a body. Liberty welcomed the Government's announcement, but expressed concern as to whether the detail of this proposal would allow all the report's recommendations – many borrowed from Liberty – to be implemented in practice. In any case, it was a stable-door-locking exercise. The horses continue to bolt. "The first duty of the police," according to the Police Federation, "is the protection of life."

I saw my lawyer Keith Taylor again. He told me that nothing much would happen for some months, if not longer, and that I would have to be reassessed yet again for permanent ongoing damage. It seemed I must appear as reduced as possible in my capabilities if I were to win any compensation, while at the same time attempting to present myself to the world as employable.

"Should I walk away from this civil case?" I asked.

"No, but the doctors' assessments are a little disappointing," Keith said, implying that I had overly impressed the doctors. By now, I had read the hospital notes covering my treatment, so remembered the Astley Ainslie psychiatrist's comments: "Her initial superficial presentation is generally very good and this may mislead others into thinking that her recovery is rather better than is the case so far."

I did not walk away. Keith Taylor did not recommend that I should. Too many people have been through a similar case to mine, or worse, and had no possibility of justice. If I end up losing the case, I thought, that result will carry its own message.

My civil case was due to come to court in the autumn of 2002, three-and-a-half years after the injury. I increasingly dreaded appearing in court. Since I retained no memory of the injury itself I feared cross-examination.

Three weeks before the appointed court date, Keith Taylor, who had been diligently building the case, called to tell me that the Met had offered to settle out of court by offering me money. "If you refuse and continue with the court case, you could receive three or four times what they're offering," he said. "Of course, if they win you'll get nothing." The amount offered would not change my life. Formally, the Metropolitan Police did not lose this case. Nor did they win it. I accepted. Coincidentally, my chronic fatigue summarily ended. "Clearly, these events are related," said a friend. Perhaps.

I now re-entered media contact books as a campaigner on police driving. I am not. But my experience augmented my interest in global road safety. On World Health Day 2004, the World Health Organization launched a road-safety campaign with the slogan "Road Safety is No Accident". They made a point of referring to "injuries" – or deaths – never "accidents". This accorded with my thinking, although my learned friend and owner of the East Lothian cottage where I began inching back to normality reminded me of the Latin root of the word, which suggests that "accident" simply means an unforeseen event and is therefore technically an accurate term for what happened.

Be that as it may, road injuries and deaths are now so common worldwide that five years after the WHO campaign, in 2009, the first ever United Nations conference addressing road safety was held in Moscow. The world has accepted a heavy price for the right to drive freely and fast. Our love affair with the internal combustion engine undoubtedly takes its toll, and we seem to accept the price that must be paid for driving around in lethal weapons. Thousands of people die every year.

Following years of campaigning by the Global Road Safety Commission, the side-effects of road-building and vehicle-use in the developing world would be tackled. I decided to go to Moscow to learn more, so registered with the press bureau, booked flights and cheap accommodation and headed east – alone. What was discussed was sobering. For instance, in Africa alone, road deaths were killing more people under 20 than malaria, AIDS and tuberculosis combined. Road safety measures – seatbelts, a ban on drinking and driving, the use of helmets when on a motorbike, and the provision of bridges and underpasses on six-lane highways – were seldom part of developing-world culture and practice. At the end of the conference, a motion was passed to instigate the Decade of Global Road Safety (2011–2020), with a goal to stabilise and then reduce the forecast level of road traffic fatalities around the world. The motivation for this event was actually as much economic as compassionate: national economies suffer beyond measure from the decimation of workforces following road injuries and deaths.

I returned to Britain, armed with sufficient argument and factual material to win a commission to make two programmes for BBC Radio 4 on the topic. The budget allowed us to visit Kenya and Costa Rica, both countries where the statistics for deaths and injuries on the roads were eye-watering. I would like to think that the resulting programmes were at least informative.

Allan had now accepted the job of Bureau Chief at the BBC's Paris office, which delighted me since it was easy and relatively cheap to visit, and full of diversions when he was working. Our lives seemed to have weathered the storms and buffets of the "unforeseen event".

Gradually, the world was forgetting my injury. When I was hired for work, it was never suggested that my contribution could or would be anything other than first-class. Politics, the arts, human rights, education – all my familiar fields of work – reappeared, and I was relieved that quality broadcasting had not died while I had been flirting with the same fate.

BBC 4 had been founded, with a documentary strand called *Storyville*. The distinguished documentary-maker Roger Graef won a commission to make a documentary with me about my experience, called *Who Am I Now?* This allowed me to visit my former consultant Dr. Richard Greenwood at the National Hospital, who I had not now seen for two years. I remembered that he did not expect me to return to earning a living. When I told him that I would be presenting Radio 4's *The World Tonight* live that evening – and he hadn't seen me for two years – he murmured "exceptional".

I was hired to present a new Saturday morning discussion-programme on BBC Radio 4, *Talking Politics*, which ran for seven years, and I was occasionally asked to present *The World this Weekend* and *The World at One* for Radio 4. Broadcasting live was now possible.

I had not looked in the mirror for a long time. One morning, Allan, on his way back to Paris, phoned to tell me that he had left his passport behind. Could I bring it to the station from where he was starting his journey? Just out of the shower, I called a taxi, pulled on a sweater and trousers and within 15 minutes was rushing through the station. As I neared him, I saw him blench. I had not had time to blow-dry my hair into its customary fringe, so my injury was clearly visible – a somewhat jagged scar across my right eyebrow, still angry-looking after years.

As I made my way back home, I resolved to investigate restorative surgery, which the National Health Service did provide since the aim was not so much to gild the lily as to protect the squeamish. The operation was done at London's Royal Free Hospital under a general anaesthetic. Although I looked like an unsuccessful prize-fighter immediately afterwards, the work settled down within a few months.

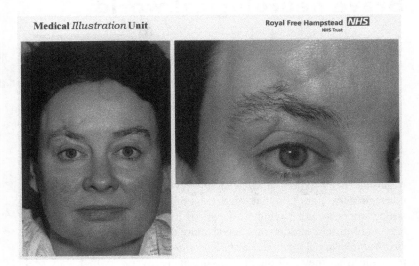

Figure 8.1 Medical illustration of Sheena's right-eye scarring
Source: NHS Royal Free Hospital

Simon Withey, my surgeon, called me in for an assessment after six months. "I can improve on that," he said. So yet again, I was under the knife. The final result is good. No horses have been frightened to date.

I began to present the annual coverage of the General Assembly of the Church of Scotland. In 2005, an online channel called Teachers TV was launched, which ran for five years. I auditioned to present the weekly news programme, and was hired.

On Christmas Day 2005, in Edinburgh, Allan and I hosted late lunch for my family. It was a traditional day: we watched the Queen's Christmas message, and played familiar family games before clearing up and sharing the presents we had bought each other. After the family had left for home, Allan and I exchanged gifts.

I cannot now remember what I gave Allan. I will never forget what he gave me. I have never taken it off the fourth finger of my left hand.

Six months later, my father married us in the Playfair Library in the University of Edinburgh.

Today, Edinburgh is home.

Chapter 9

Brave neurological world

Much has been written at an academic level about brain injury and its consequences. I am told that this field's bible is known as the "Lezak", which interests me, having read part of a work produced by Thomas Kay and Muriel Lezak, called 'The Nature of Head-Injury' in *Traumatic Brain Injury and Vocational Rehabilitation*, written in 1990. It sets out to tackle what they call the "ten myths of 'recovery'" which they seek to "debunk". I immediately identified with one of the myths targeted – that "Recovery Occurs in a Year". This myth was already out-of-date, I think, when they wrote the book. I would suggest that setting any time limit on recovery is unwise. The authorities are guarded: the Brain and Spine Foundation tells us that "as a general rule recovery after a severe head injury takes many months . . . some degree of recovery may continue for several years, especially in younger patients". I was 44 when I suffered a very severe head-injury. I undoubtedly experienced some degree of recovery for years. Twenty years on, I fancy that I am still experiencing subtle improvements – albeit indirect ones, like finally addressing my weight gain.

But I took issue with Kay and Lezak's attempts to debunk the fundamental notion of recovery.

We avoid phrases such as "recovery after head-injury". Most people's experience, and therefore expectations, regarding illness and injury is one of temporary reduction in functioning, followed by a gradual return to normalcy. People get sick, go to hospital, and get better. Bones are broken, casts are applied for a period, muscle strength regained over several months, and scars fade. When commonplace notions of recovery are applied to head injury, however, considerable harm can be done. Almost never does a patient "recover"; the residual deficits are usually significant and permanent.

The continual expectation of recovery can lead clients and families into denial, frustration, disappointment, and ever worse, extremely unrealistic expectations and planning . . . we prefer to speak in terms of hope for as much improvement as possible, to build in realistic expectations from the beginning.

Ten years after the injury, I was irritated to read this. I was working as a freelance journalist again in radio and TV. Twenty years since the injury, I have mellowed.

I do live, I know, with "residual deficits": my sense of smell is at best vestigial; my short-term memory requires a form of active reinforcement unnecessary pre-injury; my singing voice is replaced by a crow's rasping caw (a doctor recently told me that survivors of various traumas lose the ability to sing, but no-one knows why); my finger remains permanently bent.

I choose not to drive, despite holding a valid licence, since I remain nervous about my right-field vision.

Perhaps Allan's phrase "my new normal" – which I only read when we wrote this book – is my current condition. Perhaps the work I have been and still am commissioned to do is conducted within the context of "permanent residual deficits". And perhaps with the help of acquired care and caution I am living and working within my cognitive and physical means. I know what I have achieved over these years in terms of meeting deadlines and expectations, initiating enterprises and property purchases, and tackling challenges. Friends and strangers no longer refer to or possibly even remember the 1999 injury.

Neuroplasticity and cognitive reserve

Why is Sheena an exception? This is the million-dollar question that all clinicians ask. I can speculate that her personality played a central role; Sheena is self-motivated and she has a natural curiosity and thirst for knowledge. I can wonder if it was the Scottish upbringing and resilience, with an attitude of "get on with it". Is it the unwavering support of Allan, as well as family and friends? Probably all of these contribute. What about neuroscience: can it help?

In 1999, the term *neuroplasticity* was not as commonly used as it is today. In essence this is the brain's ability to regenerate and form new connections, which can be adaptive (and also maladaptive). Changes in brain function can be measured on neuropsychological tests; however, we do not know if the brain has reformed a connection (restitution), or whether a different brain region has taken on a function (substitution). Alternatively, neuroplasticity or changes in the brain can be measured by using a range of neuro-imaging techniques like functional magnetic reasoning imaging (fMRI; e.g., Reid *et al.*, 2016). Does Sheena have an extraordinary capacity for neuroplasticity?

Another possibility is that Sheena had an unusual degree of *cognitive reserve* to draw upon. In general, notions of cognitive reserve have been proposed to explain why some individuals experience better functional recovery in the context of brain lesions like TBI, or why some individuals are less affected by neuro-degenerative conditions like Alzheimer's disease. Recently, cognitive reserve has been associated with functional outcome and identified as being neuro-protective, with the suggestion that it may be a useful indicator of TBI severity and assist with neurorehabilitation planning (e.g., Leary *et al.*, 2018; Steward *et al.*, 2018).

What exactly is cognitive reserve? A number of indicators of cognitive reserve have been used, including estimated premorbid level of intelligence, years of education, occupational experience and enriching activities. Schneider and colleagues (2014) found that for individuals in rehabilitation after a moderate-severe TBI, educational attainment was a robust predictor of disability at one year post-TBI. Sheena obtained an Honours degree from Edinburgh University, which places her at a very high level, as well as having an estimated premorbid IQ in the superior range, even when in PTA, and her occupational experiences would certainly classify as enriching. Can it be that simple?

....

On the positive side, I have at last shed the excess weight gained when my appetite-control mechanism seemed to have been disabled, and am 30kg lighter; and I am no longer depressed. Both these improvements are related to the original injury's consequences. I sometimes dream again, too, after almost two decades of dreamless nights.

The minister at my father's old church preached recently on the liberating power of forgiveness. I listened intently. I think he is right. If we are brought up Christian, it is drummed into us: "forgive us our trespasses, as we forgive those who trespass against us."

In reality, forgiveness is far from easy.

The minister quoted from South African Archbishop Desmond Tutu, who has written extensively on forgiveness. He asserts that not to forgive disfigures humanity. "There is no future without forgiveness." I hear him, and I think about the circumstances he has lived through. I resolve to try to forgive. It is hard.

I try pitying bad police drivers; there are, I tell myself, a few brave good apples operating in a bad-apple police culture. I am no Christ figure. But I have no overweening desire for revenge – rather a will to see exemplary justice done in the form of an ill-trained driver owning up to getting it wrong, thereby possibly provoking an improvement in police instruction and practice when it comes to using the lethal weapon that is a car or a van.

"The police are the public and the public are the police," said Sir Robert Peel in the nineteenth century. "The police are members of the public who are paid to give time and attention to duties which are incumbent on every citizen in the interests of community welfare and existence."

I continue to strive towards genuine, heartfelt forgiveness.

I am still sometimes asked for advice by friends or relatives of people who have suffered some sort of brain-injury. They want to know what will happen, and whether and when things will get better. I always say that I am no clinician but do know that it is impossible to generalise about brain-injury. I am a second-rate guinea pig in that on paper I should be a textbook example of how certain injuries produce predictable long-term results: ongoing ataxia, loss of memory, mood-change, dependency and so on. No-one can explain why I do not conform to that expected norm.

What I can say is that one's condition can continue to improve for years, not months. The changes become perceptible largely to those who do not see one often. The safety-net of an insurance policy aided my financial health. And the support and stimulus of other people, principally Allan, was immeasurably valuable.

I have read in the Lezak book that "there is a small group of individuals who have a severe or very severe injury who do exceptionally well". What qualifies one for this clinically imprecise category, and am I a member?

Rebuilding life after brain injury

Yes, Sheena is in this category. She has done exceptionally well. She is a remarkable example for others to have no doubt that it is possible to recover many abilities and rebuild a very full and rewarding life after experiencing a very severe TBI, with all that entails.

Allan too is exceptional. He navigated the difficult and ever-shifting terrain of main carer, a role that he chose when he could have simply returned to his overseas job. He went from being Sheena's boyfriend to main carer, to partner and then husband. His insights are many and I believe his frank openness will be an invaluable source of strength for other carers too.

Neurorehabilitation is a creative and unknown endeavour that we embark upon together. You need a team; as a clinician, there is knowledge and there is instinct. Yes, it is a science and there is an evidence-base to draw upon. Yet, the neurorehabilitation process requires *experience-based intuition*. At the end of the day every person can be the one to have a remarkable recovery. Yes, it may not be the same as before, but it is possible that life can be filled with many experiences that result in a productive and joyful life. The rewards are many for those who embark on this journey.

For me, there is only deep gratitude for Sheena and Allan; they have taught me much, my life has been enriched and I hope others benefit too.

Figure 9.1 Sheena at time of writing, 2019

Source: Douglas Robertson Photography

References

Leary, J.B., Kim, G.Y., Bradley, C.L., Hussain, U.Z., Sacco, M., Bernad, M., and Chan, L. (2018). "The association of cognitive reserve in chronic-phase functional and neuropsychological outcomes following traumatic brain injury". *Journal of Head Trauma Rehabilitation*, 33(1), E28–E35.

Reid, L.B., Boyd, R.N., Cunnington, R. and Rose, S.E. (2016). "Interpreting intervention induced neuroplasticity with fMRI: the case for multimodal imaging strategies". *Neural Plasticity*, 2016, article ID 2643491.

Schneider, E.B., Sur, S., Raymont, V., Duckworth, J., Kowalski, R.G., Efron, D.T., and Stevens, R.D. (2014). "Functional recovery after moderate/severe traumatic brain injury: a role for cognitive reserve?". *Neurology*, 82(18), 1636–1642.

Steward, K.A., Kennedy, R., Novack, T.A., Crowe, M., Marson, D.C. and Triebel, K.L. (2018). "The role of cognitive reserve in recovery from traumatic brain injury". *Journal of Head Trauma Rehabilitation*, 33(1), E18–E27.

Tutu, D. (1999). *No Future Without Forgiveness*. London: Random House.

Index

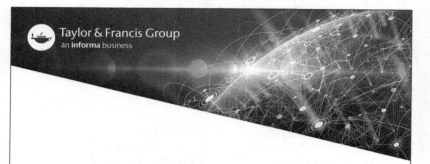